T0285757

BLACK SETTLEMENTS

— IN —

Southern Illinois

KIMBERLY FRANCE

THE
History
PRESS

Published by The History Press
Charleston, SC
www.historypress.com

Copyright © 2024 by Kimberly France
All rights reserved

Front cover, bottom: private collection of Toni Craig Garrison.

Unless otherwise noted, all images are from the author's private collection.

First published 2024

Manufactured in the United States

ISBN 9781467155595

Library of Congress Control Number: 2023946688

Notice: The information in this book is true and complete to the best of our knowledge. It is offered without guarantee on the part of the author or The History Press. The author and The History Press disclaim all liability in connection with the use of this book.

All rights reserved. No part of this book may be reproduced or transmitted in any form whatsoever without prior written permission from the publisher except in the case of brief quotations embodied in critical articles and reviews.

To the descendants of Black settlements in Southern Illinois.

CONTENTS

PREFACE

This book endeavors to document the historical contributions of Black persons in Southern Illinois. It began as a project researching my family ancestry, because my grandmother's maiden name (Allen) did not appear on her and my grandfather's marriage certificate. I did not know she had been married before. As I would later learn, no one else in the family did, either.

I knew where she grew up, because we visited often. Sundays after church were spent at her sister's house in Marion. There were scores of cousins my age who lived near my Aunt Nellie's, as there was a park next door. Every Memorial Day, we went "up in the country" to Thompsonville for a barbecue. We played in the church building, which was barely standing. We ran through the cemetery and down the hill to the outhouse. We laid flowers on the gravestones of family members. Every funeral was followed by a trip to the cemetery. We never said goodbye, because they were always with us, and we were always visiting them.

Grandmother was my name for her. My cousins called her "Grandma" or "Grandma Madelene." I remember fishing with her as a child and the joy I felt when I graduated from fishing with a pole to a rod and reel. She was not allergic to fish, but she did not eat them. "It tastes like cotton in my mouth," she said. She taught me how to catch them, clean them and cook them.

Aunt Gracie and Grandmother did everything together, since both had been widowed for years. They lived just four blocks apart. I remember occasional trips to the country to pick fruit and nuts that they would use to make preserves. I remember the visits to Aunt Sarah's (their aunt) and brushing her long hair. They taught me to crochet and play cards. I never won a game of gin rummy, but I felt like the most blessed child growing up at the feet of these beautiful, strong women.

With all of those childhood memories, I was amazed to learn that the "country" that I knew and loved was not family land, but a Black settlement that had been home to dozens of Black families. If I was not aware—and I had the benefit of the experience—then younger folks surely did not know.

When my research began in earnest, beyond my family tree, I was saddened and disappointed by the many articles published over the years that spoke of the settlement (Africa), centering it as a gracious gesture of white settlers. The stories conflicted, but none told of the Blacks who made it home. One source claimed that the settlement was built for the "negroes." Another claimed that a white man traveled to Missouri and purchased the enslaved spouse of the person he inherited and brought them to Illinois and set them free. Though the author admits that the couple ("negroes") paid for the land and their freedom "by their hard earnings," he goes on to say of the settler, "this humane and generous act…justly entitles him to a prominent place in history." That was the moment when I decided, since the true story was not being told, I would tell it myself.

I began interviewing friends, family and locals to get a fuller picture of the settlement. When trying to document the settlers' experience, I discovered that many were not confined to one place. They would marry in one county and raise a family or work in another. There was much movement, and many stories were lost due to lack of documentation. For every trail lost, a new one would emerge. There were more settlements.

Thus the idea for this book was born. It is flawed, because it is not possible for one person to know the history of all the Black families in every county. Poring through books commissioned to document history, I discovered how little mention Blacks received. Some books made no reference, while others made references in passing. Sometimes, I would peruse an entire publication to find one line, such as, "the fact remains that the white children are playing on the streets or engaging in that useful and ornamental occupation of hanging on to passing trains, while the [Negroes] go to school." A mention like this was invaluable to documenting the existence of a Black settlement and also the reason the bibliography is so long.

This brings me to the conclusion of my story and the introduction of the reader to this book. As a Black woman who grew up here, I can only tell the story from my experience. Blacks built community with three pillars: church, school and cemetery. Where those existed, there were Black settlements.

A gathering in Locust Grove, Williamson County, Illinois. *Private collection of Toni Craig Garrison.*

Though the evidence is lacking in print, it abounds in the descendants. We are the beneficiaries of their legacy, and it is our responsibility to honor them. One hundred years from now, I do not know how Black history will be curated, as the pillars have already morphed in form. While the current state of race relations remains hotly debated, the key to healing and true reconciliation lies with the reckoning that our ancestors' blood demands.

As important to promote the Southern Illinois origins of Popeye and Superman is to promote the home of Oscar Micheaux and Annie Turnbo Malone. The contributions of African Americans from the region were significant in the past and continue to the present day. It is this rich history that will inspire future generations to continue the trend.

NOTE: The terms *Black*, *colored*, *Negro*, and *mulatto* were key to my research and allowed me to identify the individuals in the book.

ACKNOWLEDGEMENTS

Although "thank you" is insufficient, I want to express my sincere gratitude to the people who have shaped this journey.

Thank you to Walter Green, for always being up for a road trip. Our families were already bonded as neighbors and friends, but the kindness and hospitality you extended to me when my mom was killed will never be forgotten.

Thank you to Meghan Harmon and Becky Quinten, for sharing your amazing research.

Thank you to Vickie Devenport, Darrel Dexter and Walter Ray of RAAHSI, for your earlier work and for sharing information without hesitation.

Thank you to Clifton Jackson and Marolyn Cowsert, for introducing me to Grayson; to Denise Drue, for giving me a tour of Lakeview; and to Sheila Simon, for letting me participate in your class trip to Gallatin County.

Thank you to Leann Johnson, for introducing me to IRAD and for your remarkable research skills.

Thank you to Laura Cates Duncan, for researching the Jackson County historical documents.

Thank you to the McDaniel family, for hosting me at the museum and allowing me to debut some of the material. It was there that I was able to connect with so many who shared information with me on Union County.

This book would not have been possible without the elders: Jackie Armstrong, Nona Taborn, Jeanne Mays, Duane Perkins, James McKinley, Edward Blythe, Wendell O'Neal, Bob Wills, Carlton Smith and Michael Green. You were so gracious with your time and wisdom to share your families' experiences.

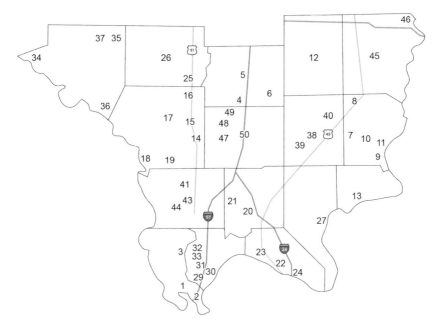

Alexander
1. Cache (62962)
2. Cairo (62914)
3. Tamms (62988) (62993)

Franklin
4. West Frankfort (62896)
5. Benton (62812)
6. Thompsonville (62980)

Gallatin
7. Equality (62934)
8. Omaha (62871)
9. Bowlesville (62954)
10. Gold Hill (62984)
11. Shawneetown (62984)

Hamilton
12. McLeansboro (62859)

Hardin
13. Elizabethtown (62931)

Jackson
14. Carbondale (62901)
15. De Soto (62924)
16. Elkville (62932)
17. Murphysboro (62966)
18. Grand Tower (62942)
19. Pomona (62975)

Johnson
20. Vienna (62995)
21. Elvira (62912)

Massac
22. Metropolis (62960)
23. Joppa (62953)
24. Brookport (62910)

Perry
25. Du Quion (62938)
26. Pinckneyville (62274)

Pope
27. Golconda (62938)
28. New Liberty (62910)

Pulaski
29. Mounds (62964)
30. America (62996)
31. Villa Ridge (62996)
32. Ullin (62992)
33. Village of Pulaski (62976)

Randolph
34. Prairie Du Rocher (62261) (62277)
35. Eden (62286)
36. Rockwood (62280)
37. Sparta (62286)

Saline
38. Harrisburg (62946)
39. Carrier Mills (62917)
40. Eldorado (62930)

Union
41. Cobden (62920)
42. Makanda (62958)
43. Anna (62906)
44. Jonesboro (62952)

White
45. Carmi (62821)
46. Grayville (62844)

Williamson
47. Dewmaine (62918)
48. Colp (62921)
49. Freeman Spur (62841)
50. Marion (62959)

Current towns proximate to Southern Illinois Black settlements. *Courtesy of Madison Stephens.*

INTRODUCTION

O ne cannot tell the story of Black settlements without first acknowledging those who came before. It is necessary to not just review history as a chronological timeline but also examine it in the context of the human condition and the circumstances that define it. Before this nation was established, Indigenous people were here. They were in Florida, when the first Africans arrived near St. Augustine. They were in Virginia, when the *White Lion* reached the shores of Virginia with enslaved people from Angola. They were in Massachusetts, when the *Mayflower* arrived. They were in Pennsylvania and Maryland, when two men were hired to resolve a territorial dispute between families. They were in Illinois before it was named. Before a man from Haiti, Jean Baptiste du Sable, sailed to Chicago, the Illiniwek tribe gave rise to the territory that is Illinois.

The American Revolution was beginning when a frontiersman left his Boonesborough settlement and headed west. Neither his story, about the man who murdered the first U.S. secretary of the treasury, nor the stories of men hired to explore the Northwest Territory, are covered in this book. Their travels through the Southern Illinois territory are noteworthy because Black men (mostly unnamed) accompanied them.

Before the United States was formed, Illinois changed hands among France, Britain and Virginia and was part of the Indiana Territory. By the time the census was taken for statehood, the American Colonization Society was created and sending Africans to the newly established nation of Liberia. The War of 1812, the Black Hawk War and the Trail of Tears would pass through Union and Pope Counties and permanently change the budding nation's landscape and devastate a population of people.

The issues of slavery and involuntary servitude plagued the nation for years. In Illinois, governors both appointed and elected alternated in their positions, though many were slaveholders themselves. One attempted to amend the constitution to allow for slavery; another freed his slaves after arriving in Illinois. Yet another favored involuntary servitude. While some historians hold a Frenchman responsible for introducing Negro slavery to Illinois, Blacks in Southern Illinois are rarely recorded as coming from outside of the United States.

Many writers of Illinois's history say the settlers brought their slaves with them to the new territory with the intention to free them after a few years of service. Black code laws denied Blacks' rights of citizenship. As a result, Blacks were shackled, chained or otherwise bound by contracts that were enforced with violence. Between 1794 and 1818, Franklin County was among the counties with the longest indenture terms, with ninety-nine-year-term indentures for women. In Gallatin, Randolph, Madison and Pope Counties, contracts ranged from thirty to fifty years.

In 1819, Illinois passed its first runaway slave law. "Every black or mulatto person who shall be found in this State, and not having a certificate [of freedom] as is required," would be prosecuted. The act prohibited slaves and free Blacks or "mulattoes" (those with one-fourth Negro blood) from staying more than ten days after entering Illinois. Announcements were published seeking the return of runaway slaves and kidnap victims, despite laws that prohibited kidnapping free Blacks. It was illegal for a Negro, Indian or mulatto to testify in court against a white person. Blacks were listed as property to be assessed. Blacks were rarely granted the respect of identity. Illinois can claim part of the Underground Railroad as routes from Chester through Sparta, Centralia North, Cairo North, Equality and DuQuoin were used by some of the three thousand souls in the "free state" who sought the basics of self-determination.

Some found freedom in Illinois. When gold was discovered in the mid-1800s, many settlers traveled to territory newly claimed from the Mexican War on roads called traces. This proved fatal for many, because modes of transportation were limited to foot, horse or boat. The Fugitive Slave Act sanctioned returning Negroes to a subhuman status. Before Samuel Blow changed his name to Dred Scott and filed suit for his freedom, he and his wife, Harriet, were moved from Virginia to Alabama to Missouri as property. The debates between aspiring candidates of the sixteenth presidency would again place Southern Illinois at the center of history, involving an issue not yet settled. One candidate wanted voters to decide their status, while the other famously said, "This government cannot endure permanently half-slave and half-free."

Tennessee seceded from the United States, and before the Civil War ended, more than two hundred Black soldiers attempting to surrender were murdered at Fort Pillow. A colonization attempt via the Île-à-Vache failed, and the issue of what to do with "contraband" Negroes persisted. Many Blacks fled New York after the draft riots. They had limited options, dispelling the myth that the North was a safe haven. The year of the drafting of the Emancipation Proclamation, which would free slaves in Confederate states, Illinois law decreed, "No negro or mulatto shall migrate or settle in this state."

1

THE BIRTH OF EGYPT

There are as many differing accounts for the origin of the nickname for the Southern Illinois region, Egypt, as for the boundaries that comprise it. Most consistent is the comparative reference to travel during the famine, when severe weather destroyed crops in the central part of the state, to the biblical story.

The boundaries of Egypt are also a source of debate. Some sources use the thirty-sixth parallel as the line of demarcation, while others use the thirty-ninth. One source claimed that everything below the path from St. Louis, Missouri, to Vincennes, Indiana, was Egypt. The focus of this book is the southernmost sixteen counties of Illinois and the people of color who settled there.

Occupations for a male head of household recorded on a census might be blacksmith, farmer, laborer, cooper or drayman / express wagon driver. For women, common listings were laundress, seamstress, homemaker or teacher. Doctors made house visits by wagon and documented conditions such as apoplexy, consumption, dropsy, Bright's disease, pleurisy and pellagra. As the industrial era emerged, the practice of "regulating" Blacks continued. Southern Illinois towns were built largely near mills, mines, railroads and factories. A factory in Jackson County began operating in 1866, and the wages were reported as follows: "$4–5 for brick masons, $2–3 for stonemasons, $3 for plasterers, $2–3 for carpenters. White laborers received $1.75 while Blacks received $1."

An 1866 map showing Egypt region in Southern Illinois.

A decision of the United States Supreme Court entrenched separation by race just as America was entering a conflict involving Cuba. Riots like those that occurred in Carterville, Eldorado, Anna Jonesboro, West Frankfort, Pinckneyville and Vienna were often prompted by racial violence. Many labor disputes often had racial undertones, and sundown towns adopted formal and informal rules to exclude Blacks from their city limits. When union workers went on strike, mine owners recruited Blacks to cross picket lines, making them the victims of more violence. In 1890, there were Blacks in every county in Illinois. By the Great Depression, six counties in the state showed no Black residents.

2

CHALLENGES DOCUMENTING BLACK SETTLEMENTS

Though Blacks were in Illinois before the United States was established, their identities remain largely unknown. Some counties maintained a slave register or book for Negroes. Official documents largely referred to Blacks merely by number or by first name. Some Blacks took the names from the people who owned them, like "Rondeau" and "Woods." Blacks' status as property confounded the issue. When people of color were ascribed a last name, there was frequently a "white" family with the same surname nearby. Spelling consistency remained a challenge.

Most Black settlement began on land where Black families farmed and lived. Identification of a Black person by last name was usually only possible when names appeared on census or marriage records. On census records, there was often an indicator of their status as free. This may have been a distinction without a difference, as these records were taken prior to Blacks obtaining citizenship. There was a common practice, however, to denote a person of color with labels such as "colored," "Negro/Negress," "Black" or "mulatto." This was more consistent on census records than on marriage records.

The 1850 and 1860 U.S. Census records were the most reliable sources of identification for several reasons. First, the 1850 Census was the first federal census taken after all sixteen counties were officially established. The census lists the name by head of household and records names in order of residence. Both censuses recorded the race of the occupants, though many people who later transcribe these records may not omit the race column. While white was the default and was rarely written, the initials *m* for mulatto, *b* for Black or *n* for Negro would appear to identify a person of color. Though these are primary sources, they are flawed.

Most census records of that time are transcribed and thus somewhat subjective. There is often conflicting data when comparing one census to the next. The census might record the birthplace of the person as well as the birthplace of the person's mother and father separately. In the event of inconsistencies, a more definitive source may not exist.

This book identifies Black settlements using the cultural markers that were most consistent and distinguishable indicators of the era: a church, a school and a cemetery. The church was the strategic institution of the Black community. In many cases, the church and school were in the same location, and the cemetery was often located on church grounds. While it was indisputable that an AME church was African Methodist Episcopal, these churches are dwindling in number, and most records are not publicly available.

The most reliable source of some Black settlements came from the AME Church's Annual Conference Proceedings. In 1873, there were churches already in existence in Carbondale, Metropolis and Shawneetown. Ten years later, the denomination is represented in Cairo, Sparta, Metropolis, Carmi, Grayville, Hodges Park, Shawneetown, Mound City, Harrisburg, Gallatin, Brooklyn, Greenville, Grand Chain, Pleasant Hills, Massac and Webster's Mill. The challenge with using this resource exclusively is that it is limited by denomination and timing.

Identifying settlements by name presented unique challenges. Black settlements' names may reflect aspirations, like Liberty, New Hope and America. Whites referred to the same areas with names considered derogatory, like Negro Salt Wells, Negro Springs, Negro Hill and Negro Town, making the presence of Blacks undeniable. In many cases, Black residents referred to the place by one name and whites by another. In other cases, the settlements were renamed when the county boundaries changed or when a post office was established or moved.

Tracing settlements by their Black settlers required understanding their movement. Because most Blacks never achieved a life of peace and tranquility, relocation was necessary. Racial violence, the promise of a job or the ability to marry or acquire land were common reasons for families to pull up roots. One historian wrote of Black residents in Massac County, "The Negro has learned of the better opportunities to the North and he will continue to leave the sedate, tradition-bound Egypt. Negro youth is reaching out for the greater opportunities which DuBois, in a militant way, advised. Our local, colored citizens are progressive, clean and energetic and have a strong desire to be successful."

Prior to 1855, schools were either private or subscription. Subscription schools contracted with parents or guardians to teach spelling, reading, writing and arithmetic for a term, usually three months. The earliest schools usually contained all ages (grades) in one room and often began in churches. The Committee on Stations, Circuits, Missions and New Work submitted the following recommendation during an AME conference: "Religion may be maintained for a long time by the mere emotional and faith support, but a religious organization must add to faith, knowledge….In the district we are making efforts to establish an institution of learning." Only after laws were passed that made schools public and free did a number of schools for Black students build separately from churches.

When describing one Black school, a recorder stated, "It would be out of the question to think of putting the children in school with the white children." Black schools bore the names Attucks, Dunbar or Douglass, after notable Black persons. Despite the spelling of Frederick Douglass's name, Douglas schools often used only one *s*. Some schools were named in honor of the sixteenth president.

Sometimes, the only evidence of a school came from an obscure note in a newspaper, such as the one that appeared in the *Daily Free Press* in Carbondale on April 1, 1899. The note referred to a teacher in the "colored school at Cairo." One newspaper reported "colored" school salaries in Pinckneyville. The colored schoolteacher made $20 a month, compared to other teachers in town, who made between $35 and $50. "The janitor at the colored school house won't get enough money to pay for soap to keep his clothes and hide clean $1.50/ month."

In the 1920s and 1930s, some schools were already integrated. When there was no separate school or cemetery for Blacks, segregation often existed within the institution, such as divided classrooms or separate burial sections. Most Black schools were not completely closed until the mid-1960s, after the two Supreme Court cases ordered school integration.

Another challenge to identifying Black settlements is the varied names used to refer to those locations. In Gallatin County, Equality is known for having derogatory names for its Black settlement. Salt Lick was referred to as Negro Salt Wells. These settlements also went by multiple names, or the names changed over time. Thompsonville's Black settlement, which began as part of Franklin County, was called Africa or Fancy Farm. Later, when

Williamson County was established and the post office was relocated, Locust Grove became the more popular name. In most cases, the settlers for whom the location was home simply called it the "country," with a familiarity and shared knowledge that was known only to those who lived there.

Not every Black settlement had an African American newspaper, as Cairo (Alexander County) did, but most newspapers reported on Black cultural celebrations. Though another state is credited with the first Memorial Day celebration, Black persons in the Locust Grove and Lakeview settlements had a long tradition of observing Decoration Day. Emancipation Day is another observance regularly practiced in Black settlements in Southern Illinois, with the first newspaper account of it in the summer of 1882. These annual observances were chronicled in Elizabethtown, Brookport and Carbondale through the years.

On August 6, 1914, one newspaper reported a celebration of the "negro fourth of July." On September 10, 1914, another reported: "Tuesday, September 22nd, the colored folks at Dewmaine will observe Emancipation Day with a big celebration. It will be a great gathering for the colored people of that vicinity." Hardin County continued its celebration but changed the name when most of the Blacks left.

Perhaps the greatest challenge in researching Black settlements is timing. County boundaries were often formed from other counties, for example, Pulaski from Alexander, Saline from Gallatin and Williamson from Franklin. The year the settlement occurred would correspond to the county of record at the time. Because most settlements are no longer in existence, this book uses the current county boundaries as well as the current towns and townships to approximate their locations. Most elements that defined Black communities are no longer in existence. The sixteen southernmost counties are listed below in the order they were established:

Randolph, October 5, 1795
Johnson, September 14, 1812
Gallatin, September 14, 1812
White, December 9, 1815
Jackson, January 10, 1816
Pope, January 10, 1816
Franklin, January 2, 1818
Union, January 2, 1818

Alexander, March 4, 1819
Hamilton, February 8, 1821
Perry, January 29, 1827
Hardin, March 2, 1839
Williamson, February 28, 1839
Massac, February 8, 1843
Pulaski, March 3, 1843
Saline, February 25, 1847

3

ALEXANDER COUNTY

The first record of Blacks in Alexander County was of enslaved and freed persons. County records identified Jane Baker as a free woman in 1816. The same year, James Smiley and Peter Grayson were offered as security for a loan in 1821, and James Pendleton was sold. Mary Anne Van Wych was freed in 1825. The 1830 Census records six slaves and six free Blacks, and the sale of Black persons continued. Wade, "a French Negro" from Cairo, was kidnapped and taken out of state in 1847, presumably to be sold. From the time that Black settlement began in the county, Black persons' actions were countered. Joseph Spencer, a proprietor who owned a boat that doubled as a hotel and tavern, was killed by a mob that also burned and sank his boat in 1855. In 1857, a man brought suit against the railroad for assisting runaway enslaved persons' escape to Canada, because his slave, Joseph, escaped in August.

By 1850, there were at least seven Blacks who were heads of households. The surnames of the Black residents were Baker, Belts, Black, Crowell, Gilpon, Hood, Hunt, Massy, Overton, Rich, Robinson, Simmons and Williams. Davie Overton is listed in household no. 92 as a Black male born in Missouri around 1746. He was the oldest recorded Black man on the census that year, at age 104; the youngest was Lucretia Black, 2, born in Illinois. Most of the Blacks who were listed on the census were born in Missouri or Kentucky. A few were from North Carolina and Tennessee. One exception was David W. Gilpon, a mulatto male, 37, born in Massachusetts.

Cairo was a crucial location during the Civil War. Island Number Ten was a small island on the Mississippi River near the Illinois line where runaway slaves were kept in protective custody by the Union to prevent slave traders and former owners from taking them south. The war, the railroad and the geographic location of this island contributed to the county's population growth.

By 1862, there were 2,200 Blacks in Alexander County, and Black settlement was underway. In 1864, a two-story, four-room frame building was erected on the corner of Nineteenth and Walnut Streets in Cairo that served as a church and school. In 1869, the legislature taxed the county for the "influx of Negroes that depend on theft, robbery, and begging for a living…more criminals and convicts than any Illinois county."

Names associated with Black settlements in the county include America, Beech Ridge, Cache, Trinity, Golden Lilly, Tolbert, Hodges Park, Sandusky, Tamms and Idlewild. Beech Ridge was four miles north of Cairo on Highway 3. Cache was settled when the post office relocated there from Beech Ridge. America began in Alexander County when the county seat was moved. In Trinity, another name for Cache, there was a church on the east side and a school east of the railroad tracks. Farther east and north of Cairo was Golden Lilly, also known as Tolbert, which lies between Highway 51 and Interstate 57. It was home to the Chapel of God Church (AME), also known as Ward Chapel AME.

In 1878, the AME conference appointed Joseph Perkins to the Cairo circuit. Churches operated schools as well, presumably in the same building. The Cache Negro Baptist Church dissolved into the "Egyptian Consolidated School." Farther north of Cairo was Hodges Park and Sandusky, which is located just south of Tamms, formerly known as Idlewild. Beech Ridge and Cache were absorbed as part of Cairo. Two cemeteries were part of these settlements, Cairo City Cemetery and Beech Grove Cemetery.

South Center School was uncovered in the records, but its location is unclear. Douglas School was originally built as a high school in 1864. At some point, it was converted to a grade school (Douglas Elementary) and remained so until the 1965–66 school year, when a referendum consolidated ten schools into three. The Douglas School building stood on Walnut Street between Douglas and Fourteenth Streets. Other schools built to educate Black students were Washington Elementary (1872), Bruce Elementary (1900), Sumner High (1926), Garrison Elementary (1941) and Washington Junior High (1941). Other school names mentioned include Promised Land and Alexander County High (also known as Sandusky

High). Cairo also had a Black grade school, St. Columbia Catholic, which opened in 1928.

Cairo had two Black newspapers, *Three States* and the *Gazette*. *Three States* ceased publication in February 1883, and William T. Scott published the weekly *Gazette* starting in 1888.

On February 19, 1900, mob violence broke out in response to the lynching of a Black man named John Pratt. This led to twelve men being indicted, but in July, all were acquitted. Lynchings of Blacks and whites continued, often resulting in the presence of armed guards in the county. One of the more famous protests against segregation and discrimination occurred at a swimming pool in Cairo in the 1960s. In 1865, Cairo's population was 24 percent Black. Between 1910 and 1920, two thousand Blacks were said to have left Cairo as a result of violence. By 1960, African Americans made up 38 percent of Cairo's population.

4

FRANKLIN COUNTY

There are conflicting accounts of the origin of Franklin County. "Slavery of the colored man once existed in the territory of which Franklin County is now composed," wrote one historian. Accounts differ both on the timing of settlement and the settlers themselves. According to some sources, the settlement known as Africa or Fancy Farm was settled for Blacks by a white man who brought his enslaved persons to Cave Township between 1804 and 1818. The 1818 Census shows this man with one free person of color listed in his household. In 1820, this same man is listed having four free persons of color in his household.

The Illinois State Census of 1818 and 1820 tell a much broader story. The 1818 Census shows a total Franklin County population of 1,329, of whom 52 were free and 15 were enslaved persons or servants. The same census lists the following Black heads of households: Elijah Burnes, Stephen Burnes, Wm Burnes and John Grey. The 1820 Census records Samuel Ford and Solomon Russle as Black heads of households. That year saw a total county population of 1,775, with 67 free people of color and 7 enslaved persons or servants. The number of French Negroes and mulattoes held in bondage in 1835 and 1840 was 5.

Another source credits Richmond Inge and Silla McCreery as the county's first Black settlers. Though the accounts differ, the gist is that this couple was purchased from slavery in Missouri and brought to Illinois. Richmond Inge (also Eng and Ing) and Tilla McCreery appear in the same household in the 1850 Census and living next door to Chas McCreery, who was born in Illinois in 1831. Inge is reported as born in Virginia about 1805 and Tilla (aka Cillar or Priscilla) born in Kentucky around 1795. The family history told by the white McCreerys places Silla's arrival with the family in 1816.

The oldest Black resident in the 1850 Census is a male, Amy Carter, age seventy-five, born in Missouri. The youngest is one-year-old Prince Albert McCreery. Surnames of Black residents in this census are Carter, Caster, Inge, McCreery and Stockton. The 1860 Census contains only Blacks and mulattoes with the last names Allen, Gray and White. No Black persons are recorded on the 1870 Census in the county. The likely reason is that Blacks were simply located in the area now considered part of Williamson County.

Evidence of further Black settlement and its demise appeared in newspaper reports and county history. In H.M. Aiken's *Franklin County History*, he writes:

> *My uncle took the negro boy to Benton and turned him over to the sheriff as there was a heavy penalty for assisting a fugitive to escape to Canada yet he sympathized with the negro boy. The sheriff placed the Negro boy in jail and advertised the runaway Negro. After so many days the owner failed to call for his property. The boy was declared a "free man of color." The boy was hired and taken to Springfield, where he worked in the State Capitol. The Negro lived to be an old man, and died only a few years ago in the city almost a stone's throw of the home of the "great Emancipator."*

The *Benton Republican* reported in 1923, "Benton Illinois flirted with barring blacks during the day by sending a note to the Franklin Hotel 'givin the colored help warning to leave town within a certain length of time.'"

Coal mine explosions killed dozens of Black strikebreakers between 1905 and 1909. During a United Mine Workers of America (UMWA) strike in 1920, whites rioted against Sicilians and forced the mine owner to fire Blacks who had been hired as strikebreakers from Kentucky.

The only evidence of a Black settlement in Franklin Heights is a mention from a local newspaper that described construction of the one-room school by pressing a discarded side-door Pullman railroad car into service. The October 1, 1919 article stated, "Franklin Heights has a school for negroes, six students," and named the teacher. Other sources state the existence of a Black settlement in Freeman Spur, with little details.

5

GALLATIN COUNTY

Gallatin County is one of the counties that maintained a slave register. The courthouse contains transcripts of ownership, which record the counties from which the enslaved were brought. In some cases, Blacks were freed as consideration for past faithful service or in exchange for money. In many cases, they were indentured for years of hard labor in salt mines. The county courthouse is also home to a mural commissioned in 1941 that depicts the Indigenous Americans who pioneered the salt production for which the county was famously known.

Slavery and indentured servitude in the county was documented as early as 1824 with the recording of William Killis, a mulatto man, age twenty-five, who was indentured on July 5, 1814. A Negro woman, "Silvey," also twenty-five, was recorded on June 22, 1815.

The census of 1818 distinguished free and not free Blacks only by number, not name. Slaves and servants were not separated. At the time, the county's total population was 3,856. About 320 were Black, of which 89 were free. In 1820, the total population declined to 3,451. Of these, 337 were Black, and 98 of these were counted as free. Only two Black heads of households appeared on both census documents. Isham Cheek is listed as Isem Cheach in 1818 with 3 free people of color in his household; in 1820, he is listed with 8 free people of color.

James Hood had eleven free people of color in his household in 1818 and five in 1820. Other Blacks, as they appear in the record, are as follows: Lucy Anderson, Ben C. Brown, David Brown, Stephen Burns, Obid Copeland,

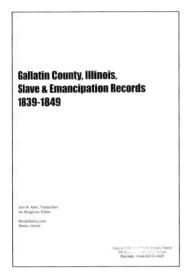

Gallatin County, Illinois,
Slave & Emancipation Records
1839-1849

John W. Allen, Transcriber
Jon Musgrave, Editor

IllinoisHistory.com
Marion, Illinois

Eldorado Memorial Public Library District
PO Box --- --- ---- Street
Eldorado, Illinois 62930-0428

Page from Gallatin County Slave & Emancipation Records, Gallatin County.

Jarri Davis, Ths Dawson, Jeffrey Deprest, Sam Ford, Silnah Killes, Jessee Michael, Daniel Norante, Benjamin Straton, Clary Robinson and David Whimsey.

The trail from Hopkinsville, Kentucky, to the Saline Salt Works in Illinois made kidnapping a constant threat, not just for those who were in Kentucky but also for those in Illinois who were unable to secure or prove their freedom. Jepthah Hardin was indentured in Gallatin County on December 12, 1815. Venus, born in South Carolina around 1795, was taken to Kentucky and sold. She was later indentured and moved to Shawneetown. She sued for her freedom and won it on June 23, 1832. She married William Ewing on August 7, 1836. William Bird (Byrd), a Black cooper born in Kentucky, lived with his family in Equality precinct. He was fifty-four. His wife, Jane, and children were listed as mulatto. He moved with his family from Logan County, Kentucky, to Shawneetown in 1831.

In 1826, a man ran an announcement in the *Illinois Gazette* offering a handsome reward for the return of his runaway or kidnap victim. In 1828, Joe Allen went to Gallatin County Court to prove his freedom. In 1830, Clara Robertson posted her emancipation bond. Nelson "Fox" Perry was indentured to the "salt king" in 1829. He should have been released in 1840 but instead was arrested and sent to the state penitentiary in Alton. The children of Benjamin Fauver from Shawneetown were kidnapped in 1849.

A Black man named Andrew Jackson published his account as a runaway enslaved person who was captured in Gallatin County and sold at the county's slave auction in October 1840. He was sold and transported to Bloomington, Illinois, eventually making his way to New York via his family in Wisconsin. Other accounts mention Henry Brown, sold in 1832, and Isaiah and William, sold in 1833. The latter two are said to have escaped. Frederick Clements escaped slavery in Kentucky and arrived in Gallatin County in June 1857. On August 1, he was returned to slavery by court decision.

In 1842, two families immigrated to Liberia from Gallatin County. They were the family of Reverend Bryant Smith and the family of Caesar Leaper. The Smith family left after their children were kidnapped.

Some would not know their fate when they arrived in Gallatin County, only the certainty of what they left behind. James T. Jackson, a free Black man, came to Gallatin County from Tennessee. Maria and Patrick Henry were fugitive slaves sold in Virginia who made their way to Gallatin County. In 1862, two contraband families were brought to town to work on a farm. On September 1, 1862, Ms. Sanders was said to be the last enslaved person to be registered in the county. She was considered contraband and was hired to work in Cairo during the Civil War.

Robert Wilson, a farmer, was born to Aaron and Queenie (DeBall) Wilson in Kentucky in 1834. Before his father died in 1848, he and his family moved to Illinois. In 1859, they moved from Equality/Shawneetown to Williamson County. Robert served in the Twenty-Third U.S. Colored Infantry from October 9, 1862, until May 31, 1863. He farmed land until he died in 1887.

James Madison White, son of Peter and Elizabeth Violet White, was born on a farm near Equality on July 23, 1863, and died at age seventy-eight. He was the son of an enslaved man who was kidnapped and taken to Equality to the Old Slave House. His father married a "colored woman" from Equality, and James was one of their twenty-four children.

At one time, Gallatin County had the most Blacks in Egypt. Black settlements in the county were confirmed in Bowlesville, Equality and Omaha Townships. Cornelius "Neal" Elliott and Aaron Wilson Sr. are credited among the early Black settlers in Gallatin County. Beyond the township names, other names referring to Black settlements included Cypressville, Cypress Junction, Half Moon Lick, Redwood Point, Round Pond and New and Old Shawneetown.

Elliott arrived in the area in the 1820s. His children were born between 1829 and 1853. Other settlers are Henry and Laura Baker and Howard Towles Elliott, who worked the Saline mines from 1827 to 1847. When Neal Elliott died in 1868, his estate papers identified the following heirs: Peter (born December 10, 1829), John (May 17, 1832), Charles H. (January 24, 1835), Minerva (March 15, 1840), Sarah (February 24, 1842), Eary (August 28, 1845), Mary (January 11, 1847), Samuel (1851) and George A. (1853).

The 1850 Census noted a total county population of 5,448, including 153 colored males and 200 colored females. The 1860 Census records the oldest Black residents as Louis Caldwell, an eighty-six-year-old male born in Tennessee; and Malinda Taylor, an eighty-four-year-old female born in Virginia. The youngest were Virginia Root, Lacey Price and Samuel Stewards, all two months old. Blacks recorded in the 1860 Census include the following last names: Akers, Allen, Archer, Arington, Baker, Barger, Bell,

Blue, Briggs, Bunkin, Byrd, Caldwell, Carroll, Casey, Chocley, Cooper, Craig, Curry, Darby, Day, Dimerck, Eddy, Eliott, Ewing, Farber, Fletcher, Forrister, Greer, Hardy, Hefford, Henry, Higgins, Hubbard, Jacobs, Jefferson, Johnson, Jones, Keaton, King, Kinsall, Martin, McAllister, Murrell, Portee, Porter, Prater, Price, Railer, Rawlings, Rucher, Scott, Sellers, Shelby, Sherwood, Shockley, Smith, Steward, Stewart, Taylor, Thurman, Toles, Vincen, Ward, Washington, White, Whitesides, Wilson, Wiseheart and Wilson.

The county is best known for Hickory Hill (aka Old Slave House), which lies one mile south of the intersection of Routes 1 and 13. The house was built in 1838 by a man who owned three salt furnaces and held a government contract for salt making. Much lore surrounds the "Salt King," who was indicted for kidnapping and selling enslaved persons but was never convicted. In 1851, the man and his wife deeded a lot to trustees of Concord Old Side Baptist Church for People of Color on the north side of Lane Street between Walnut and McHenry Streets.

Some of the earliest Black churches in the county were Presbyterian. One was located east of old Route 13, also known as Slab Road. Black Presbyterian churches faded due to the lack of Black Presbyterian ministers and the rise of AME and Baptist churches. The Colored Emancipation Baptist Church sent representatives to a church convention in 1843, and the church established a building in 1844, when a white church transferred property to AME trustees.

Gallatin County regulators organized in part to drive out Blacks. One historian records that Reverend Jordan W. Early, a bishop of the AME church in Shawneetown, was attacked by an angry mob in 1861. The AME conference appointed C. Holmes to the Shawneetown circuit in 1878. Trustees of a white Presbyterian church leased their old building to Black residents for a church and school to establish a Black nondenominational church in the 1870s.

Schools were documented in Omaha and Equality. In Omaha, a subscription school existed in 1820, with Pros Robinson as the teacher. The teacher for the Gold Hill School was not named. Equality had Dunbar School, with George W. Tanner as the teacher. Dunbar School, located in Bowlesville Township, operated grades 1–4 and 5–8, until it flooded in 1937. As times passed, the one-room schools were phased out, and all Black children were required to attend Dunbar School. Those families living too far away in the county for their children to walk to school moved to Shawneetown.

Circumstances of the specific Black settlements and their decline are unknown. In 1861, the county charter read, "All free white inhabitants of

Above: Salt pool in Equality, Gallatin County.

Opposite: Shawneetown marker, Gallatin County.

the city [Shawneetown] who were residents of 6 months were to be legal voters." Despite the denial of rights to Blacks, many risked their lives to serve in the Civil War. Residents of Shawneetown listed as privates in Company D of the Twenty-Ninth Colored Infantry during the Civil War are: James M. Bell, John S. Day, Cornelius Elliott, Timothy A. Guard, Peter Levell, Samuel Marshall, Elias McCallister, James H. Patton and Jefferson Taburn.

6

HAMILTON COUNTY

Herbert K. Russell's book *The State of Southern Illinois: An Illustrated History* relays the following story indicating Black settlement in Hamilton County.

> *An old colored man, an entire stranger, made his appearance and announced himself as a preacher. Of course no excuse would be taken and the old man had to preach! He did so and preached the first sermon ever preached in Hamilton County. This sermon of the old colored man pleased the people so well that they determined that he should teach them at a school....In a very short time, the colored preacher was engaged in training or teaching the first school ever taught in the county.*

Jesse Hardesty, born in 1785 in North Carolina, made his home in Hamilton County. He married Hannah before 1818, and she died in 1821. He then married Sarah Cross, and she died in 1898. Jesse died and his will probated in 1850. No Blacks with the last name Hardesty appear in the 1850 Census, and it is unclear if he is the man mentioned in the story.

George Ward recorded his freedom with the court on March 31, 1841, and Simon Wheeler was recorded on August 30, 1841. No people of color with the name of Hardesty appear in the 1850 Census.

Only three surnames appear in the 1850 or 1860 Census that were listed as mulatto. These were Clayborn, Nash and Scott. The oldest in the county was listed as Anna Nash, age sixty; the youngest was William H. Scott, five months.

In 1866, a county school report listed a separate colored school as "the first that took cognizance of the colored pupils as a separate class." There were four Blacks in the county under the age of twenty-one; by 1870, there were twelve. The school was likely housed or run by the church, as the residents believed "religious and moral training should go hand in hand with the training of the intellect." Scott Harrison is the only "colored" minister mentioned as part of the Concord ME Church.

PEOPLE OF COLOR EXTRACTED FROM 1860 FEDERAL CENSUS, HAMILTON COUNTY

NAME	AGE	GENDER	RACE	BIRTHPLACE
Clayborn, Ellen	38	F	Mulatto	VA
Clayborn, Harvy R.	27	M	Mulatto	AL
Clayborn, Joel	5	M	Mulatto	IL
Clayborn, Louiza J.	7	F	Mulatto	IL
Clayborn, Martha A.	2	F	Mulatto	IL
Nash, Anna	60	F	Mulatto	VA
Nash, Catharine	15	F	Mulatto	IL
Nash, George	22	M	Mulatto	VA
Nash, John	65	M	Mulatto	VA
Nash, Sarah J.	28	F	Mulatto	VA
Nash, Stalen	20	M	Mulatto	IL
Nash, Susan	26	F	Mulatto	VA
Scott, Caroline M.	35	F	Mulatto	?
Scott, Isabell	4	F	Mulatto	IL
Scott, James M.	15	M	Mulatto	?
Scott, Malinda	20	F	Mulatto	?
Scott, Micajah	20	M	Mulatto	TN
Scott, Sarilda	3	F	Mulatto	IL
Scott, Serina	1	F	Mulatto	IL
Scott, Sophrona A.	10	F	Mulatto	IL
Scott, Stephen	12	M	Mulatto	IL
Scott, William H.	5 mo.	M	Mulatto	IL

7

HARDIN COUNTY

The settlement in Hardin County is not named, but it likely started on the farm of John Files, east of Highway 1 on Ford's Ferry Road. By 1850, the census records approximately eighty Blacks living in the county, with the following last names: Baker, Barker, Caldwell, Field, Fields, Granes, Graves, Guard, Kark, Kirk, McCollister, Mitchell, Stewart, Strader, Stuart, Sumner, Walker and White. The oldest Blacks recorded in the census were Nancy Strader, seventy-two, born in North Carolina; and Eda Baker, sixty-nine, born in Maryland. By 1860, additional names were Burnett, Files, Kirk, Mercer and Winston. The oldest of these persons was Winna Kirk, age seventy-seven, born in Virginia; the youngest was one-year-old Jas E. Burnett. Later, Frankie Woods and Clarence Tote were fixtures in the community. They were employees of the Rose Hotel and lived behind it.

The first documented Emancipation Day observance in Illinois was in Elizabethtown on August 8, 1882. All indications are that the settlement ceased to exist by 1940. "Because the negro population has decreased greatly since 1882, the name of the annual observance has been changed to Hardin County homecoming."

Dunbar School operated from 1878 to 1938. The *Hardin County Independent* ran the following headline on May 12, 1938: "School for Negroes Closes after 60 Years." Mr. Rowld was named as the school's first Black teacher. He was from Golconda in Pope County. Vietta White Duncan (husband Carl Duncan), the teacher for the previous eleven years, said enrollment had dwindled to one student for the upcoming school year.

8

JACKSON COUNTY

Blacks were recorded in Jackson County as early as 1816, when the county was formed. A man registered his servant, Janae, for fifty years on August 26, 1816. The 1818 state census recorded 1,392 people in the county, with no free Blacks and 53 enslaved persons. By 1820, the population was 1,567, with 24 enslaved persons, and "there is but one free person of color in this county, a male over 21 years of age." In 1830, there were 40 free Blacks and 22 enslaved in households. The (free) Black heads of households were: Aaron (no last name), Wiley Chism, Woodson Chism and Barney Stewart. The next census added the following Black heads of households: Thomas Akin, Louisa Brown, Turner Brown, William Cully, Dunbelly (likely James Wilkinson Dunbaly), Patrick Mitchell, James Reed and William Reed.

In 1880, the youngest Black resident in the county was thirteen-year-old George Liggins. The oldest was Philip G. Loving. He was eighty-two and a physician. He was in the county by 1870 and settled in Carbondale by 1880. He unsuccessfully sued the Illinois Central Railroad (ICRR) for $10,000 for being thrown from a train.

Jackson County is home to several Black settlements, in Carbondale, Elkville, Grand Tower, Hallidayboro, Murphysboro and Pomona. Decoration Day was celebrated in Elkville as early as May 1888. Emancipation Day was celebrated on July 28, 1888. In Carbondale, Frank B. Jackson is credited with starting the annual Emancipation Day observance, in 1911, and it continued until 1954.

BOSTICK

The Bostick Settlement was formed in 1866, when brothers Hardin, Stephen, Dudley, Burton and William Bostick arrived in Illinois after completing their military service in the Civil War. In 1871, Washington Bostick purchased a farm; Hardin and Stephen did so a year later. The farm was five and a half miles southeast of Murphysboro in Pomona and was the site of the cemetery and school. Charity Bostick, Grace Bostick and Thomas Stoner were among the teachers at Bostick school.

Hardin Bostick and his wife deeded land for a church and cemetery. The names recorded were Pleasant Union Baptist Church and Freewill Baptist

Left: Stephen Bostick gravestone, Pomona Bostick Settlement, Jackson County.

Below: Bostick Cemetery sign, Jackson County.

Church. Though the church and school are long gone, the cemetery remains. Adolphus Isom is buried in Bostick Cemetery. The last interred is believed to have been Zachariah Lightle, born in 1883. He died on May 19, 1959. Jukes is another name reported for a cemetery located north of the Bostick Farm.

Many of the Bostick children married and moved to other Black settlements. Grace Bostick went on to teach at Douglas in Murphysboro. In 1913, she married Harry Williams and moved to another Black settlement in Elkville. Ellen Bostick married Bert Alexander and is buried in Oakland Cemetery in Carbondale. In 1905, Dudley and Lavina Bostick sued the City of Murphysboro after their son James was killed by a Murphysboro police officer.

CARBONDALE

Carbondale reported no Blacks in the 1855 and 1860 Censuses. By 1865, the census showed 96 Blacks in Carbondale of the city's total population of 1,127. By 1880, there were 422 Blacks listed by name and occupation in the census. The last names were as follows: Ailver, Alexander, Allen, Anderson, Asberry, Augusta, Bates, Binum, Bird, Bond, Bonns, Boots, Bradshaw, Brown, Burrell, Butler, Campbell, Carter, Cherry, Clark, Clemce, Curtis, Dudley, Easick, Everheart, Gaines, Gaters, Gooseberry, Grayson, Green, Guinn, Hall, Harris, Hayes, Henderson, Holland, Hopkins, Hunter, Irving, Jackson, Jenkins, Johnson, Jones, Kinner, Knowles, Lawson, Liggins, Loving, Marbley, Merriweather, Miles, Miller, Mitchell, Murphy, Omstead, Parker, Paschal, Perkins, Price, Reese, Richardson, Ringo, Rogers, Russell, Scruggs, Shaw, Shurd, Smith, Stevenson, Suttler, Thomas, Thompson, Toney, Vaughan, Vaughn, Wallace, Washington, Williams, Woods, Woodward and Wright.

Bethel AME was first organized by Reverend Ranson Grief in 1864. The church was located on North Marion Street and was then relocated to a second site, on the west side of the railroad, for three years before a building was erected at 316 East Jackson Street in 1883. Charter members were Isaac and Kate Clemons, Maranda W. Wilson, Spencer and Lucy Davidson, William Marbury, Louisa and Samuel Asbel, Wyatt and Mahala McKenna and Collin Wilson. Samuel Hutchinson became minister and teacher in 1868. In 1878, the AME conference appointed W.M. Lee to the Carbondale circuit.

Olivet Freewill Baptist Church began sometime between 1858 and 1866. After 1905, the church was located at 409 North Marion Street and then at 310 North Illinois. Rockhill Missionary Baptist Church began in Union County before moving to Carbondale in 1871 under Reverend Grayson. The current structure at 219 East Monroe was built in 1920.

Hopewell Missionary Baptist Church was founded by Reverend J.P. Brown in 1901 and was first located at East Jackson and North Wall Streets. Fire destroyed the building, prompting another move. The current building at 400 East Main Street was erected in 2001.

East Side School started inside the Freewill Baptist Church. The first standalone building was constructed in 1871. In 1906, it was named Attucks. Attucks consisted of both a grade school (402 East Main Street) and high school (410 East Main Street). A new structure was built in 1915, and the school, whose mascot was the bluebird, operated until it closed in 1964.

Edward Blythe was born in Carbondale and educated at Attucks schools. "The teaching profession was important to the [Black] community. Teachers were highly respected along with clergy, and the teachers were interested in the students' success both academically and in the community." Blythe has fond memories of the faculty and staff, who showed "genuine care and concern" at his alma mater. They include Luella Davis, Joseph "Doc" Russell, Willie D. Anderson, Mrs. Warren, Mrs. Crim, Mrs. Bowers, Lucille Walker and Thelma Walker. Edward said, "Every spring, there was a school picnic at Giant City State Park."

Edward Blythe graduated and then attended SIU. Walt Frazier was recruited to SIU in 1964, when Blythe was a freshman. "At that time, the NCAA did not allow freshmen to play varsity." Edward Blythe and Charlie Vaughn were two Blacks on the team. Edward recalls traveling with the Saluki basketball team, looking for places where Blacks could eat during conferences. He recounts an incident in which a teammate from West Frankfort proposed bringing food back to the hotel for them. His coach replied, "We all eat or none eat," and they moved to another restaurant.

Michael Green, born and raised in Carbondale, recalls his experience matriculating through Attucks schools. He was in the sixth grade when Thomas School was built. Attucks often used books discarded from Carbondale Community High School (CCHS). Green walked home every day for lunch, because Attucks did not have a cafeteria. After high school, he went into the U.S. Navy and returned to Carbondale in 1975.

Bob Wills, another Attucks alumnus, also recalled going home every day for lunch. "The East Side of Carbondale was self-sustaining...there

Duchess Club, Jackson County, circa 1950. *Left to right*: Grace Edwards, Pearl Wright, Madelene France, Liz Scott, Bertha Mitchell and Liz Carter.

was no slum property." Wills named several Black businesses that operated when he left Carbondale in 1957, including a store, a gas station and a dry cleaner. His brother James was a Marine Corps veteran and retired engineer who worked for NASA at the space center. Bob returned to Southern Illinois and settled in Carterville after retiring from the largest ocean container company. He currently serves as president of the Spirit of Attucks and recently reopened the Eurma Hayes Center, a cultural fixture in Carbondale's Black community. The accompanying photo depicts members of the Duchess Social Club, many of whom were business owners in the community.

The Attucks school song is as follows:

> *Attucks! We love old Attucks. We love her grounds and her building too.*
> *All here are fine and steady and her teachers all are ever brave and true.*
> *Rah! Rah! Rah! Her sun is always shining. Her skies are always blue.*
> *Attucks! We love old Attucks. We raise our voices in lofty praise.*

Long may you live and prosper. And your students will your flag of honor raise.

Rah! Rah! Rah! Attucks, beloved Attucks, arrayed in honor you're brave and true.

Attucks! We love old Attucks. And we hope to ever love you too.

The Black settlements of Elkville and Hallidayboro were established around 1867 by Blacks who came from Georgia to work at the mine. Elkville's Black school was built in 1897 and operated until 1932. Douglas School was located on the corner of First and Ashley Streets. The principal, Carl Lee, operated

Death certificate for Ethel Allen burial in Carbondale, Jackson County. The cause of death is listed as "by a gun shot wound by the hand of J.H. Allen, her husband."

it from 1936 until the school closed in 1966, when it joined the Elkville grade school district. Lee was an alumnus of Douglas School (class of 1916). He also taught in Colp from 1928 to 1936 and is credited as the founder of the Dunbar Society. The Williams brothers owned Williams Garage and Tractor in Elkville. Grace (Bostick) Williams is buried in Grear Cemetery. Henry Guy pastored a church there and is buried in Holliday Cemetery.

Murphysboro had Douglas School, which operated from 1885 to 1966 in the area called "the flats." The school began in a house before it was moved near Old Route 13 and Route 127 South. In 1897, a permanent school was erected in a brick building. It was named Douglas and included all twelve

Death certificate for James Allen, burial at Mt. Carbon in Murphysboro, Jackson County.

grades. Dr. Alexander Lane, who previously taught in Carbondale, became the principal and was assisted by Adeline Tony (Toney).

Another source reports a school in the Douglas School District at 325 South Ninth Street, where the first building was erected in 1892. Additions and improvements were made in 1912, 1927 and 1948. The school reportedly closed when students were sent to other schools in the 1960s. Black churches in Murphysboro were Shiloh Baptist Church and Mt. Gilead Baptist Church (founded 1914). An April 1916 newspaper article mentioned a Black school in the Ward School District in DeSoto Township. The school was officially dissolved in 1951.

Henry Bates, a Civil War veteran, settled in Murphysboro with his wife, Ellen, and their children. He was a trustee at the AME church in 1891 and is buried in the Black section of Tower Grove Cemetery, where Samuel Dalton, another Civil War veteran, is also buried.

Jackie Armstrong was born in Murphysboro in the 1940s and attended Douglas School. In the seventh grade, she moved with her family to Carbondale and attended Attucks, where she graduated in the class of 1960. Armstrong was an only child, and her parents came to Southern Illinois from Mississippi. Her grandfather Landon Armstrong had a farm that is now the site of the SIU School of Agriculture.

Lincoln was a school in the Black settlement in Grand Tower's Douglas School District 153. The school was located on Second Street, and its first teacher was Turner Randall (1895–1938). Carbondale's newspaper, the *Daily Free Press*, reported on May 27, 1899, "The Grand Tower school board has employed the following teachers for the coming year…Turner Randall, teacher of the colored school." Grand Tower is home to Walker Cemetery.

Other schools in Jackson County were integrated: Millhouse (aka Butterbush); Davis Grade School (aka Dowell Rural School), as evidenced by a 1929 class photo; and Crowell School in District 99.

9

JOHNSON COUNTY

Despite laws that were aimed at stopping the spread of slavery, county records confirm the trafficking of human beings. The earliest Black person in the county was recorded in 1813, before the county was formed. "Hannah, a negro girl…is ordered to be hired out." In 1815, Anna, a "negro girl," was purchased from an estate.

The 1818 Census lists James Hawkins as the only free Black person in the county. John Johnson is listed by name. There were twenty-four slaves or servants counted, but they were not named. The county taxed Blacks as property, with the statement, "the 9 negroes at $1.00 each." Between 1818 and 1828, five Negro boys were recorded as sold with land to one individual. In 1832, Harry, a colored man, sued to prevent his master from taking him out of the county for sale on June 7, 1832.

On April 19, 1837, Sam Hardison sued for his freedom. He was freed on May 13, 1837, and he recorded his status in Pulaski County on July 14, 1845.

The 1850 Census of Johnson County lists only two names of people of color, Elliot and Bess. All seventeen individuals listed in this census are recorded as mulatto. The oldest is Milby Elliot, a female, age fifty-six. The youngest is a five-year-old boy, James H. Bess (possibly a member of the Bass family from Union County). Other Blacks mentioned as residing in the county are the Murrell family, the Allen family, S.T. Oliver, William Lathem and R. Thomas.

History points to Black settlements in this county in Vienna and possibly Elvira. Negro Knob and Sand Cave were located a few miles west and north of Miller Grove.

The Wheeler family arrived in the county sometime after 1865. Green Wheeler was recorded as a minister in the Black church in Vienna. Green Valley Cemetery was a burial place for Blacks. The February 1906 issue of the *Vienna Times* tells the following story.

> *Another dead infant has been found in our town. Last Thursday a dead baby was found in the home of James Green (colored) living near the colored Baptist Church on the south side of town. It was placed behind the door and covered up with some old quilt and proved to be the child of Minnie Reese, a colored living in the same house with the Greens. Coroner Hood empanelled a jury and after the investigation, the verdict was that the child, which was newly born, had lived, but had been killed in some manner by the mother and she is being held on a murder charge and will be taken to jail as soon as she is able to be removed there.*

Before the Civil War, a Negro boy who worked at a hotel on Third and East Main Streets was accused of theft. He was hanged and beaten until he died. The hotel proprietor's wife later confessed to taking the money. The homes of some Black families in Vienna were burned on September 6, 1954, and the people moved. As late as 1999, the "colored church" was still standing on the south side of Seventh Street.

10

MASSAC COUNTY

The earliest records of Blacks in the county documented servitude or emancipation. Tenoe was freed on October 5, 1829. Rhoda was hired out for twelve months in 1849. Richmond was freed on December 14, 1849. Washington Chaves (Chavis) was freed on May 17, 1851. That year, the county saw its first case involving the kidnapping of a Black person. Henry Barret was freed on August 12, 1853, and several court cases document people charged with harboring or bringing Negro slaves into the county as late as 1864.

The 1860 Census records 112 free Blacks in the county, with the following last names: Perkins, Chavis, Vose, Sellers, Stewarat/Stewart, Neuban, Farmer, Moreland and Rogers. The oldest resident was forty-five-year-old Henry Stewart, and the youngest was one-month-old William Sellers. At one point, Blacks composed 20 percent of the county's population. By 1950, it declined to 3.7 percent. The Black settlements with the highest numbers of Black residents were in Metropolis, Brookport and Joppa, with a smaller number in Mermet and Black Bottoms. Names referencing Black settlements were Brooklyn for Metropolis and Robinsville and Baptisttown for Brookport.

Bellgrade was the Black settlement near Metropolis and Choat, located off US 45, east of State Highway 145 and Interstate 24. One historian wrote: "Bellgrade community was the home of a Negro man named Brown who was convicted of killing two Brookport women with an axe. Brown paid for the crime with his life. He was the last man hanged in Massac County." This was likely William Brown, who was reported hanged in the jail yard on December 16, 1927.

Massac County's Black churches were well documented. The First Baptist Church (Metropolis) was established in 1866. Ferdinand Robinson served as pastor for twenty-seven years. Reverend Henry Willet purchased land to form the Brookport Bethel AME Church on December 28, 1871, with Everett Trumbo, Robert Tinsley and Lewis Burton as trustees. Early member families included Childress, Hawkins, Young, Allen, McGood, Johnson, Sims/Simms and Wheeler. Because fire destroyed the original structure, in 1891, another frame building was erected. It also burned. Another building was constructed during the administration of Reverend Speese. In 1917, the building was completed, and a cornerstone was laid by Reverend J.E. Reddick, pastor. The church had many pastors over the years, with some returning a second time, such as Reverend J.H. Fisher, who arrived in 1907. He stayed a long time and returned in 1940. He died during his pastorate. J. Sidney Tate was pastor from 1958 to 1959. He returned in 1963. Elmer Simms, Hiram Simms and Carl Lowery were the trustees. Services were conducted under the direction of A.L. Robinson. In 1965, Elmer Simms was ordained, and he served until his death in 1980.

In 1875, the Little Rock Christian Church was formed. Reverend Macon served as pastor. Joppa was home to the Clover Leaf Baptist Church and Cumberland Presbyterian Church. Both Mount Hebron Baptist Church and a Presbyterian church were located in Choat.

In 1904, both the Antioch Baptist Church and the Freewill Baptist Church were organized. S.S. Cousins was associated as pastoring the latter. Some Black residents attended the Church of God on Johnson Street. The AME Church appointed G.W. Peyton to the Massac circuit, and one of its churches, St. Paul AME Church, was located on the west end of downtown. Three churches were established in the county in 1913.

In Brookport, Charles M. Curry and James K. Brown served as pastors at some points. B. Milton Cooper was named as pastor of First Missionary Baptist Church.

United Baptist Church was organized in 1914 with J.M. Young as pastor. He was replaced by J.B. McCrary. The deacons were Isaac Moore, James Baker, Henry Flowers, Aaron Green and Frankie Howard. The mothers of the church were Eliza Baker, Mary Flowers, Josie Moore, Matilda Blackwell, Ella Flowers and Lula Landers. Lawrence James also served as pastor of this church.

As the population in the Black settlements dwindled, the churches pooled their resources. Zion Baptist Church ceased operating in 1900. Soon after, Nineveh Baptist Church and Goodman's Chapel followed. In Mermet, the

Church of Christ, the Methodist and the Presbyterian churches shared a building on alternating Sundays. When Reverend Macon pastored at Siloam, that church, Shady Grove and Little Rock took communion together every three months.

New Hope in Baptist Town was near the first railroad crossing entering Brookport. The pastor was Reverend Dehoney, who resigned in 1912. When the small frame building was destroyed by fire, the congregation worshiped in the home of James Baker. The deacons decided on a joint church meeting with another church, and in 1913, Baptist Unity Church was formed with the merging of the two congregations, pastored by Rafield Sanford. Pastor J.H. Roulac and Reverend Lenus Turley were associated with multiple churches. Sanford was associated with St. Paul AME and Brookport AME Churches. Reverend Turley conducted part-time services at Joppa Clover Leaf Baptist Church and pastored for seventeen years at Brookport Unity Baptist Church. He was also the namesake of Turley Park in Carbondale, Jackson County, Illinois.

According to George W. May, "School teaching is the principal Negro profession." There were three Black schools in the county. Oak Grove was a rural school built a half mile northeast of Choat. Herschel Owens, a local policeman, was an alumnus of Oak Grove. Dunbar Elementary and High School operated from 1921 to 1953 in Metropolis. Lincoln High School later consolidated with Brookport.

Metropolis, like Cairo, had a Black newspaper. On March 4, 1898, J.B. McCrary began the *Metropolis Weekly Gazette*. He went on to publish it for thirty years. The Colored Baptist Church Society also produced a publication, the *Baptist Truth*, from Metropolis.

Oscar Micheaux was the fifth child born in his family on a farm near Metropolis in 1884. After working for about a year as a Pullman porter, he relocated to South Dakota in 1904. Between 1919 and 1937, Micheaux wrote, directed, produced and distributed approximately thirty films with all-Black casts. Paul Robeson is said to have made his acting debut in a Micheaux production in 1924. Micheaux's prolific film and book career earned him a posthumous star on the Hollywood Walk of Fame in 1988. He died in 1951 and is buried in Charlotte, North Carolina.

11

PERRY COUNTY

When the census was certified in 1825, there were forty-seven free people of color in the county. The 1860 Census lists Blacks by name: Farrell, Mann, Muypat and Washington. The oldest resident was Sarah Nancy Mann, sixty. The youngest was Francis R. Washington, two months.

The Black settlements in the county were in DuQuoin and Pinckneyville. The area where the Pinckneyville settlement was located was referred to as the "black hills." A photograph of the house that was formerly the Black school appears in the book *Sundown Towns*. Blacks were driven out in 1928. The *Waterloo Republican* published the school staff and salaries on June 22, 1899.

> *The crop of teachers over at Pinckneyville is plenty, and cheap, judging from the salaries paid. The principal of the schools there will draw the munificent salary of $50.00 per month for the coming term and the next prize winner gets $40.00, followed by eight others at $35.00, and winding up with the teacher of the colored school at $20.00. The janitor of the central school will get a salary of $30.00 per month and the favored individual who had "pull" enough to catch on the job of janitor at the colored school house won't get enough money to pay for soap to keep his clothes and hide clean $1.50 a month.*

Between 1916 and 1950, most of the Blacks in Perry County were concentrated in DuQuoin. Most were buried in the Independent Order of

Death certificate for Rockford Stewart, burial IOOF Cemetery in DuQuoin, Perry County.

Odd Fellows (IOOF) Cemetery. DuQuoin was one of the few settlements to have a Black physician. Zephaniah Green lived in DuQuoin. He was the town's only "negro doctor," Other residents were businessmen Pete Thompson and Will Bolden. Ed Owens, a mulatto, was a Black mail carrier.

Lincoln School "housed all negro students" from 1910 to the 1960s. The Afro-American Protective League of Illinois, the state branch of the National Equal Rights League, was a Black self-help organization that convened a conference in 1898 to support school cases in Alton, Centralia and DuQuoin.

Smith Memorial AME Zion Church was established in 1879. The congregation changed the name of the church to honor its founder and first pastor, Reverend William Smith, after his death. The church moved to a new building at Park and Maple Streets about 1923 after a tornado destroyed the prior location. Other Black churches and pastors included Mt. Zion Baptist Church (Elijah Holmes), Free Will Baptist (Grandpa Berkely), Mt. Olive (Elder Winston) and St. Paul Church.

In her book *It's Good to Be Black*, Ruby Berkely Goodwin chronicled the experiences of her family in DuQuoin in the early 1900s. Ruby, the daughter of a coal miner and teacher, wrote:

> *Dad's people had to come to DuQuoin from Island Number 10 shortly after the close of the civil war (mid-1865), a small island on the Mississippi River near the Illinois line where runaway slaves were kept in protective custody by the union government to prevent slave catchers and former owners from taking them back south. His grandmother Judy, [was] a slave.*
>
> *Mother's father, Elijah Holmes, was set free by will when his master died. He courted Sara Ann on a nearby plantation. Elijah became a minister, and when they were invited to DuQuoin for a revival, they decided to settle there. Elijah sent for his daughter Sophia from Mississippi. Braxton met Sophia and married her. Holmes was pastor of the Zion Baptist Church.*

The book mentions St. Paul Baptist Church and three members: Deacon Tinsley, Elder Ross and Reverend Stuart. Also mentioned are Elder Winston and S.D. Davis of Mt. Olive Baptist Church. The Berkely family left DuQuoin in 1920.

12

POPE COUNTY

The earliest record of Black residents in Pope County was on November 26, 1816: Jeffery, thirty, a Negro in Golconda. Judith, age seventeen, was recorded in 1817 as indentured for ninety-nine years. The Pope County Deed book lists free papers to Sally and Frances in 1821 and Joshua Scott in 1827. One man freed twelve enslaved persons in August 1823. An estate probated in 1829 ordered the sale of two enslaved persons, Macklin and Frank.

In the 1830s, "Mr. Sides and his wife of Pope county…were attacked and brutally knocked down in their house, $2500 in gold of the money of a freed slave taken, and the house set on fire.…And so began an 18-year's civil war between the Regulators and Flatheads, unsurpassed in the annals of Illinois history."

The number of "French Negroes" and mulattoes held in bondage in 1835 was two. Kidnapping stories of Blacks in Pope County involved the family of Patrick Henry Alsup. Another record mentions Elijah Morris. "A free colored man, Elijah settled about 2 miles from Golconda with his family of 4. In 1843, there was a raid on his home and his children were kidnapped."

The earlier census, of 1818, did not distinguish free, servant or slave. Blacks were simply counted as people of color. The last names of Black residents in the census are as follows: Alsup, Bowlin, Caldwell, Dabbs, Dimnery, Ellison, Field, Goins, Gowen, Gowers, Hill, Jones, Miller, Monly, Moore, Oliver, Rameua, Randeau, Roberts, Scott, Shepherd, Sides, Simpson, Singleton, Smith, Spoon, Still, Sumner, Sutton, Tanner and Williams. Of the approximately two hundred Black residents recorded, the oldest in the county was Sarah Monly. She was recorded as one hundred and born in Virginia. The youngest resident was one-month-old Permelia Caldwell.

Pope County was home to at least two Black settlements, one in New Liberty and the other in Golconda. The settlement known as Miller Grove has a cemetery of the same name now under management by the National Park Service. It began with the arrival of Bedford and Abby (Gill) Miller in 1844. The Williams family arrived later. Bedford deeded the land for Mt. Gilead AME Church and accompanying school, which was one-fourth of a mile north of the cemetery. In 1918, the frame building burned, and a new church was built.

Activities of Blacks recorded in the county include a Masonic lodge and a band led by Mac Pryor. Joel Stewart married Agga Taborn (Taburn) on January 5, 1859, in Pope County, but they made their home in Locust Grove. On September 10, 1863, Harrison Miller (colored) married Julia Moore (colored), and the couple remained in the Miller Grove settlement. *Ghost Towns of Southern Illinois* author Glenn J. Sneed names a Black man, Richard Fowler, as the postal carrier for New Liberty, but there are no records of a separate church or school there. "An old Negro man named Richard Fowler carried the mail from the landing to the post office. 'Uncle Dick Fowler' as he was affectionately called."

Glendale was the Black settlement located in Golconda. It was also known as Bay Bottoms. "Most of Bay Bottoms from the bridge in Homberg to Route 145 was owned by Black people." This settlement was formed when the Hill family arrived and purchased land in the Temple Hill area from the bridge to Route 145. Taking the name Sydes (Sides), in 1830, they crossed Hayes Creek and settled north of Glendale. Abraham Sides had a cluster of farms in 1844 near Glendale. Ed Woods was the custodian at Golconda School for many years. One minister, perhaps Jeremiah Sheppard, reportedly served the AME churches in Miller Grove, Elizabethtown (Hardin County) and Golconda. Most schools in the county were integrated, including Normal, Temple Hill, Sumner and Bay Valley.

13

PULASKI COUNTY

Because Pulaski County was formed from Alexander County, the records of early setters are dated after 1843, though earlier settlements, like America, already existed (approximately 1818). Nancy Burnet and Nath Burnet, both forty-five, are the oldest Black residents in the 1860 Census. Anna Burnet, ten, was the youngest. Barnet, Burnet, Green, James and Scott were the names of the Black families.

Pulaski County had Black settlements in Grand Chain, Mound City, Mounds, Olmsted and Ullin. Grand Chain's AME circuit consisted of Grand Chain, Pleasant Hills and Massac. Mound City National Cemetery, established in 1862, is where many Civil War veterans are buried. But the Methodist cemetery was known as the Black cemetery in the settlement. First Baptist was established in the 1920s, and the Pentecostal Church of God formed in the 1940s. Black students attended Forest View and Century High School.

One historian writes: "Colored people in Mound City are supporting 4 churches: First Freewill Baptist Church NW in the city, Second Freewill Baptist Church near Main Street—Reverend George Young, Methodist Church—Joseph White, Missionary Organization—Charles Moore."

In 1860, the Black population in Mound City was less than thirty. Beechwood was one of seven railyards also known as Mound City Junction or Mound Junction. The AME circuit was represented by Webster's Mill, White Chapel and Village Ridge Churches in 1873. The AME conference appointed R.S. Demming to the Mound City Circuit in 1878. The frame building of Mound City AME Church was erected in 1915. Reverend Speece and Joseph White once served as pastors there. First Free Will Baptist Church was located in the northwest part of the city, with Nelson Ricks its pastor. Later, Second Free Will Baptist Church formed on Main Street. Because of its location, this church was also referred to as Main Street Freewill Baptist Church. George W. Young once served as pastor. To avoid confusion between the two churches, the first Free Will Baptist Church was also called the Bethlehem Free Will Baptist Church or the Lovejoy Free Will Baptist Church. The Missionary Organization rented Second Free Will Baptist Church for meetings.

Lovejoy Grade and High Schools were the early Black schools in Mound City. They were named after the murdered abolitionist from Alton, Elijah Lovejoy. The school was adjacent to the courthouse. In 1919, Mound City High School was built. The accompanying image is a photo of the school and a brick from Lovejoy School when it was demolished.

The settlement developed despite the violence that settlers faced. A story involving Grand Chain and Mound City concerned Nelson Howard, a Negro man. He allegedly shot and killed someone at a train depot in Mound City on July 4, 1883. A group of people went to Grand Chain, where he lived. Howard was arrested and jailed in Mound City. The next day, a larger mob broke him out of jail and hanged him without a trial. His death certificate was not located. He may be buried in the Grand Chain Cemetery, north of Highway 37.

Only a few miles apart, residents like the O'Neal family often traveled among the settlements. Wendell O'Neal's grandfather Reverend William O'Neal was born in Clarksville, Tennessee. In 1890, at age fifteen, he left home and headed north, settling in Illinois. His grandparents met in Olmsted and raised their family. Wendell's parents, Mr. and Mrs. John O'Neal Sr., were teachers and taught their children in school: Ernest, Willie, Angelo, Clyde and John Jr. Wendell was born in Mound City. His mother also taught at Washington Elementary in Olmsted. His grandparents lived next door. His grandfather is buried in Thistlewood Cemetery in Mounds.

Wendell and his brother John Jr. were active in the civil rights movement and were part of the Student Nonviolent Coordinating Committee (SNCC). Wendell recalls the events of the summer of 1962. The SNCC field secretary came to Southern Illinois University–Carbondale. A group that included Charlie Steptoe, John Jr. and Wendell O'Neal met with Pastor Ramsey at Ward Chapel AME Church.

Photo of Lovejoy School and a brick from the school, Pulaski County. *Private collection of Edward Blythe.*

When Blacks were refused service at a local restaurant, several sit-ins followed. Demonstration sites included the skating rink and the Cairo swimming pool. Rather than integrate, the pool was filled with concrete, prompting more sit-ins. John O'Neal Jr. and Charles Neblitt were present with John Lewis at the swimming pool demonstration, which turned violent. Charles "Chuck" Neblitt joined the civil rights movement after the incident in Cairo and was one of the founders of the SNCC Freedom Singers.

America may have been another name for the settlement in Mounds. It is not clear whether the references to America were used after the formation of Pulaski County. Sneed mentions America as a site of racial tensions when a flatboat was burned that "sold whiskey to the slaves." It was also known as Boar/Bear Creek Bottoms. Residents worshipped at Graham Chapel AME, St. Paul AME, St. John Missionary Baptist and Pilgrim Rest Baptist Churches. These churches were likely located on the same grounds as Spencer Heights and Thistlewood Cemeteries.

John Lewis at swimming pool sit-in, Cairo, Alexander County. *Private collection of Wendell O'Neal.*

America Grade School may have been the original name for Douglas. It was located at 416 North Oak Street. Douglas Grade School District No. 6 was built in 1929 after the frame building burned. Douglas High School was built in the 1940s. In 1950, the Douglas basketball team was the first Black school team to join the Illinois Athletic Association. The Redbirds were coached by "Doc" Wilson. Both schools closed in 1968 after a reorganization.

Front Street was the economic center of the Black settlement in Mounds. The Chambliss family was one of the early settlers. The elder Chambliss came from Kentucky and worked in a mill in Cairo. His son Haywood was the village trustee and owner of a general store. Gwendolyn Chambliss was the principal at Douglas School.

The Chambliss general store was located at 226 Front Street, and Ben Savage had a barbershop there as well. Today, a museum at 216 Front Street preserves the Black history. In 1939, Dr. A.L. Robinson and his wife, Hazel, a nurse, moved to Mounds. He served as the town's physician and surgeon. They were members of St. Paul AME. Dr. Robinson died in 1984 and is interred at Green Lawn Memorial Garden.

Ullin was founded in 1867. Union Grove Cemetery is one mile east of Tamms, between Mill Creek and the Missouri Pacific Railroad on Tamms Road. The cemetery was segregated, with Blacks occupying rows 1–21. It is the final resting place for many Black veterans of the Civil War, World War I and World War II. Ullin Cemetery holds gravestones for the Dumas and Clemmons families.

The Black settlement in Olmsted was started by the Cross family when Christopher Cross and his son Alexander purchased farmland in 1866. Other settlers in the 1860s were Joseph Carr (Garr), Charles Davis and Andrew Radford. Caledonia was laid out after America was abandoned.

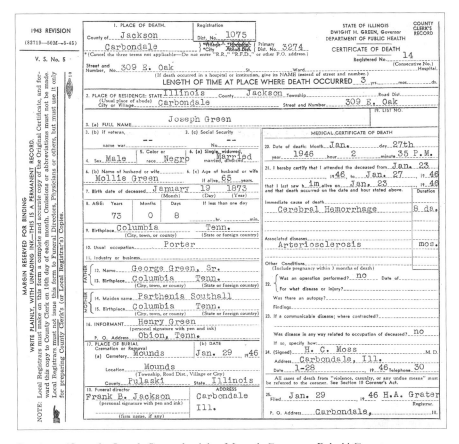

Death certificate for Joseph Green, burial at Mounds Cemetery, Pulaski County.

Olmsted was once called Caledonia. Hazel Phillips was from Olmsted. She was the second wife of M.D. Easton, whom she married on March 29, 1937. She died in 1942.

The Mt. Zion community may have lent its name to Villa Ridge. Also called New Hope, Villa Ridge was located on Highway 51 west of Mounds. Villa Ridge was home to the Mt. Zion Missionary Baptist Church and a school called South Center. Reverend A.J. Johnson built the Villa Ridge Colored Baptist Church on his farm. He was born a slave in Clark County, Kentucky, and came to Illinois in 1857. His first stop was Mound City. For seventeen years, he pastored the Villa Ridge Colored Baptist Church.

Conflicting sources cite Villa Ridge School as Lovejoy Grade School and Lovejoy Freewill Baptist Church with New Hope as an alias. Caledonia Freewill Baptist Church is recorded as the Baptist church in Olmsted.

Death certificate for Alonzo Allen, burial Ullin Cemetery, Pulaski County.

Reverend Wilson pastored Baptist churches in Olmstead, America, Grand Chain and Mound City. One of them may have been named St. Mark Baptist Church.

The first documented school in Camp Pulaski began in 1882, when land (one-quarter of an acre) was deeded to trustees of Township 16 for the colored school, also known as Hayes School. The Black teachers were C.V. Lane and Wren Harris.

The village of Pulaski was laid out in 1855. Edith's Chapel was home to Perkins School in rural Pulaski County, near Boar Creek Bottoms. Though not specified, Bethlehem, Century High, Forest View and Sumner High were Black schools in Pulaski County.

14

RANDOLPH COUNTY

In 1720, Negroes were 40 percent of the Randolph County population, at 240. Today, the first capital of Illinois, Kaskaskia, has a total population of 14 and no postal zip code. Blacks were first identified by name in Randolph County around 1818. Maria, "a free black woman," bought a parcel of land in Randolph County for sixty-six dollars.

Like Union County, Randolph County maintained a Register of Negroes. Randolph County had ninety-nine-year indenture contracts. Lydia and Jane began serving their indentures in Springfield Township on June 1, 1802. Aspasia, a woman of color, was born in 1806 in Kaskaskia and sold. She later sued for her freedom.

The 1818 census shows a total population of 45 Blacks, with 2 enslaved persons or servants in households. By 1820, the county's total population was 3,533, of which 342 were Black. Black persons listed by name were John Bacchus, Antoine Cato, Sillis Edgar, Daniel Porter and Ferrander Terrango.

The 1850 Census lists the following last names for Black families: Alaird, Allaire, Amos, Barbeau, Beauvais, Bienvenue, Bowman, Bridmier, Buatte, Campbell, Chappelle, Crawford, Deville, Fayre, Foster, Gaston, Gillis, Harris, Howard, Humphrey, Jeandron, Joiner, Jones, Kane, Labouch, Lameur, Lamure, Mary, Maxwell, McAlpin, Menard, Mitchell, Mina, Morris, Morrison, Mosby, Niswonger, Owens, Pierre, Porter, Raine, Roberts, Strother, Thornton, Urchie, Williams and Wright. The 1860 Census lists these names: Baptiste, Boone, Bridges, Brown, Croban, Douglas, Duncan, Fulton, Gaston, George, Howell, Hunter, Jackson, Lafleur, Lakenan,

1. PLACE OF DEATH	Registration	STATE OF ILLINOIS — COUNTY CLERK'S RECORD
County of Randolph	Dist. No. 7614	Department of Public Health—Division of Vital Statistics
Menard — Township/Town/Village/City	Primary Dist. No.	STANDARD CERTIFICATE OF DEATH

*(Cancel the three terms not applicable—Do not enter "R. R.," "R. F. D." or other P. O. address).

Street and Number, No. Southern Illinois Penitentiary

Registered No. 1 (Consecutive No.)

Ward, _____ Hospital
(If death occurred in hospital or institution, give its name instead of street and number.)

2. FULL NAME Everett Allen

(a) Residence No. _____ (Usual place of abode) _____ St.; _____ Ward, _____
(If non-resident, give city or town and State)

Length of residence in city or town where death occurred 1 yrs. 9 mos. 17 ds. How long in U. S., if of foreign birth? yrs. mos. ds.

PERSONAL AND STATISTICAL PARTICULARS	MEDICAL CERTIFICATE OF DEATH
3. SEX: Male	16. DATE OF DEATH January 5th, 1931 (Month)(Day)(Year)
4. COLOR OR RACE: Black	17. I HEREBY CERTIFY, That I attended deceased from Nov. 8th, 1930, to Jan. 5th, 1931, that I last saw him alive on January 5th, 1931 and that death occurred, on the date stated above, at 9:37 A. m. THE CAUSE OF DEATH* was as follows:
5. SINGLE, MARRIED, WIDOWED, or DIVORCED (Write the word): Single	Tuberculosis Meningitis
5a. If Married, widowed or divorced HUSBAND of (or) WIFE of	(Duration) (about 4 yrs. mos. ds.)
6. DATE OF BIRTH February 14th, 1892 (Month)(Day)(Year)	Contributory (Secondary)
7. AGE: Years 38, Months 10, Days 21. If LESS than 1 day ___ hrs. OR ___ min.?	(Duration) yrs. mos. ds.
8. OCCUPATION OF DECEASED (a) Trade, profession or particular kind of work Laborer	18. Where was disease contracted, if not at place of death? Do not know
(b) General nature of industry, business, or establishment in which employed (or employer)	Was an operation performed? No Date of
(c) Name of employer Sou. Ill. Pen.	For what disease or injury? Was there an autopsy? No
9. BIRTHPLACE (city or town) Sparta (State or Country) Illinois	What test confirmed diagnosis? Clinical (Signed) Louis J. Smith , M. D.
10. NAME OF FATHER Ed Boone	Address Chester, Illinois
11. BIRTHPLACE OF FATHER (City or Town) Chester, (State or Country) Illinois	Date January 5th, 1931 Telephone 92 R2
12. MAIDEN NAME OF MOTHER Unknown	*N. B.—State the disease causing death. All cases of death from "Violence, casualty, or any undue means" must be referred to the coroner. See Section 10, Coroner's Act.
13. BIRTHPLACE OF MOTHER (City or Town) Unknown (State or Country) Unknown	19. PLACE OF BURIAL Cremation or Removal Cemetery Caledonia	21. DATE Jan. 8th, 1931
14. INFORMANT C. W. Veith (P. O. Address) Menard, Illinois	Location Sparta . (Township, Road Dist., Village or City) County Randolph State Illinois
15. Filed Jan. 5th, 1931 Everett Geurin Registrar. P. O. Address Menard, Ill.	20. UNDERTAKER A. A. Lynn (personal signature with pen and ink) Lynn Bros. (firm name, if any)	ADDRESS Sparta, Ill.

Death certificate for Everett Allen. Burial at Caledonia Cemetery, Sparta, Randolph County.

Millender, Montgomery, Ricard, Shepperd, Talbot and Watson. The oldest Black resident was William Williams, ninety; the youngest was Catherine Roberts, one month old.

Black settlements in the county were in Eden, Prairie du Rocher and Sparta. Other references documented were Crow Knob, Negro Knob and Sand Cave. Bethel was the church of the settlement. The Burlingame house in Eden was said to be part of the Underground Railroad, as many abolitionist activities occurred there. The Liberty Party was an antislavery

Death certificate showing alias. The name given is Joseph Curotte, and the alias is listed as Allen. It is unclear if the name was chosen or given to the person. Randolph County.

organization founded in Albany, New York, in 1840. The Southern Illinois chapter of the organization held a three-day convention in Eden and Sparta, October 6–8, 1847.

Though the names of the school, church and cemetery were not found, there is no doubt of the existence of a Black settlement in Prairie du Rocher. "Negro-French is the common language of this town." One author wrote: "Because there was a large population of Negro citizens in Prairie du Rocher there was also a one-room Black school built, with all eight grades, taught by one teacher. These negroes had French names—Pascal and Choutau, for example. The school closed after WWII when the residents moved away and found employment elsewhere."

In Sparta, the Black settlement (possibly called Columbus) was between James and Church Streets, where the church and school were located. Vernon School started in 1870 in the AME church. In 1878, the AME conference appointed Wm. J. Davis to its Sparta circuit. The church in Sparta was named after Bishop Vernon. In 1912, a separate building was erected, and the school was relocated to James Street. Emma Holmes was a graduate of Vernon School. She and her husband, Gilbert, whom she married in 1934, were both teachers at Lincoln and Vernon Schools. Vernon School operated until 1963 and was demolished in 1997.

According to *Ghost Towns of Southern Illinois*, Rockwood Township, also called Jones Creek, was a stop on the Underground Railroad. The author goes on to say that Rockwood and the village of Jones Creek "were the head terminals." The island soon was called Liberty Island, and Jones Creek was Liberty. This was because of its proximity to the Mississippi River at the intersection of Jones Creek and Masker's Island. "The island was the first free soil Negroes, fleeing from Missouri set foot upon."

Sources differ on the names and timing. One source claims Rockwood was named in 1857. Another says that Rockwood and Jones Creek were the same location. Jones Creek established a post office in 1830 and changed the name to Rockwood in 1865. Riley Lake may have been another reference name for the area.

15

SALINE COUNTY

Saline County was home to the most talked about Black settlements of the region. Despite the numerous efforts to document this important history, some events remain largely unknown. Black settlements in the county were named Lakeview (Carrier Mills), Grayson (Eldorado), Ingram Hill (Harrisburg) and South America.

The 1830 and 1840 Censuses show 24 Black people in four households. By 1880, there were 128 Black people in thirty-one households. The 1850 Federal Census names Allen, Bell, Cole, Doage, Elliott, Evans, Guard, Mattingly, Morgan, Pumphry, Robinson, Taborn and Wilson. The oldest Black resident at the time was Pumphry Taborn, seventy-five. The youngest was William Morgan, two months. Joseph Cole filed his free papers and settled in Lakeview before 1840. He was listed in the census as born between 1804 and 1810.

In 1855, the following names were listed with only Negroes and mulattoes in the household: John Allen, Samuel Anderson, Henry Blackwell, William Carter, Aaron Elliott, Cornelius Elliott, Allen Evans, Lowell L. Evans, Richard Evans, Zach Evans, Adolfus Guard, George Holly, Jas Jackson, John Kittinger, Goerge Lee, Enoc Sewart (Stewart?), Lidda Swinna, Dorson Taborn, Bird Taborn, John Weber and Cornelius Wilson.

On October 25, 1862, a group of county residents met and decided to notify people known to bring contraband Negroes into the county for labor (in competition with white labor). The plan was to remove them or have them face destruction of life and property. This practice continued until 1870.

Before the mines were operating in 1900, the principal industry was tobacco farming, and Saline County was home to the highest tobacco production in Southern Illinois. In 1890, a strike resulted when the white men opposed the rate the Black workers were being paid. They decided to strike to force the owners to fire the Black workers. This event was told by John and Lucyella Foster in *Saline County A Century of History*:

> *Webber's tobacco stemmery employed both white and black to remove 2/3 of the stem from the leaves. The job paid about 25 cents per day. The average day's work was under 200 pounds. The biggest tobacco stemming race was between a negro and a white man. Both of them stemmed over a thousand pounds of tobacco in a day, but the Negro beat him by about sixty pounds. Some negro stemmers agreed to work for 40 cents per hundred pounds. When the white men heard of the deal, they struck and forced the tobacco companies to fire the negroes. The blacks then left town.*

The first settlers of the Grayson (Greyson) settlement in East Eldorado were likely descendants of Cornelius Elliott, as Saline County was created from Gallatin County. Neal Elliott ran an inn in 1829. The settlement, negatively referred to as Negro Hill, included Elliot's land between First Street and Dewey Road. Charles Elliott (March 31, 1833–November 9, 1887) died at fifty-four years, seven months and nine days and is buried on the land where he lived. The cemetery is referred to simply as the Elliott Graveyard. A member of the Jemison (Jamison) family is also buried there and has a gravestone that is partly visible.

Marshall Easton began his family in Grayson as well. He married his first wife, Sarah Jamison (Jemison), in 1890. They raised their family in Locust Grove (Williamson). After their divorce, Easton married Hazel Phillips, and they settled in Harrisburg.

Henry Allen and Matilda Stewart married in 1901, when their families were residents

Opposite, top: Gravestone of Charles Elliott, Grayson (Eldorado), Saline County.

Opposite, bottom: Gravestone of Lewis Jemison, Grayson (Eldorado), Saline County.

Right: Street sign, Grayson Road, Grayson settlement, Saline County.

Below: A 1990 Census record for Jefferson Douglass Alston household, Saline County.

in the settlement. Tilda, as she was called, was one of eleven Black students in Eldorado's school. They were studying with white students. According to the teacher, the Negroes did not want to go to the Black school, but then the city superintendent hit Tilda, who was eighteen at the time, in the head with a poker and "knocked her flat." This was one of several incidents of racial violence that forced Black residents to leave Eldorado. Henry and Tilda relocated to Locust Grove (Williamson) to raise their family.

Jefferson Douglas "J.D." Alston was born in 1862 and arrived in Eldorado from Tennessee. Alston (also spelled Austin and Aulston) married ParaLee (also listed as CoraLee) in 1882 in Eldorado. They had four surviving children, Lewis/Levis (born 1883), Blaine (1888), Naomi (1889) and Toussant (1891), and are recorded in Eldorado on the 1900 Census.

Peter Green was the pastor of the AME church in Grayson when plans were made to open a Black school in the settlement. The school, which was years in the making, was patterned after the Tuskegee Institute. The Eldorado School was the second of its kind—an agricultural and technical institute. It was also a historically Black college (HBCU).

THE ELDORADO NORMAL AND INDUSTRIAL INSTITUTE

More than fifty newspaper articles chronicle the rise and fall of this institution. Officers were named and a board was formed, and a charter was obtained from the state in January 1900. Initially, the plan was to request an appropriation from the state legislature, but the board decided to secure funds from an endowment rather than ask for state aid. The land and buildings were secured as a subscription school with the support of the Cuba Libre Industrial Association. The school was located on Dewey Street, across Highway 45.

J.D. Alston was chosen to lead the school for life, and the board filed for incorporation in Springfield on January 5, 1901. President Alston opened the school on March 4, 1902. On May 29, a mob stoned the house of Reverend Peter Green, and he was told to leave town. The mob also attacked the school and the homes of several Black residents. Windows were smashed at the school, and shots were fired into some homes. The first commencement exercises never occurred, as students and teachers left town, fleeing mob violence. According to the article "Race War in Illinois" in the *New York Times* of June 17, 1902:

Another attack was made last night on the home of the Reverend Peter Green, pastor of the African Methodist Episcopal Church at Eldorado. The crowd told Mr. Green to leave town in 24 hours, under penalty of death. He defied the mob and stood at his gate with a shotgun, threatening to shoot the first madman who molested him. The anti-Negro crusade has at last aroused the respectable white element, and an effort will be made to induce the colored people to reopen the Normal and Industrial School.

The board of trustees appealed to Governor Richard Yates for protection. Principal Lott and President Alston said that the sheriff told them to leave Eldorado, and he refused to deputize Black residents as deputy sheriffs to guard the school and other property. The governor replied both to Alston and to the sheriff. The *Inter Ocean* newspaper of Chicago, Illinois, on July 8, 1902, published the text of the communications from Yates to Alston and to the sheriff, Baxter.

My Dear Sir: I am in receipt of your letter of the 5th inst. In reply to mine of the 3d. I have also before me your letter of the 17th ult. I note carefully all that you say in both letters. You deny that you advised any one to leave your county, and assert that you have done and are now doing all that is necessary to protect life and property and personal rights. I sincerely hope your statements are correct, and that the report of the assistant adjutant general was erroneous, but to put it very mildly there are several things which indicate that you certainly have fallen short of your full duty in this matter. You seem to have been relying somewhat upon the United States deputy marshal to perform some of your duties and you utterly failed to respond to my request that you indicate the parties that have left and invite them to return, with assurance that you will protect them. My demand upon you in this particular was explicit, and I shall not make it again, but proceed to communicate with those parties myself as rapidly as I can locate them. Richard Yates.

In am in receipt of your favor of the 1st lost., in which you say that you are now at Metropolis because your wife decides to get away from a place that would endanger her of your life, and in which you further state that you owe $500 upon the Eldorado property, which could have been paid had you been allowed to close the school year, and at the close of which you state that the trustees have agreed to re-establish the school elsewhere, and inquire whether I have any suggestions to make.

BLACK SETTLEMENTS IN SOUTHERN ILLINOIS

In reply I will say that I suggest you return to Eldorado and open your school at the proper time, exactly as if no disturbance had occurred, with the assurance from me that I will furnish you by telegraph all such force as may be necessary to protect you and all inmates of the school from disturbance of any kind whatsoever. I note your statement that the inmates of your school lived in this state for the most part are residents, and that they were not students from Kentucky.

One newspaper reported that the Afro American Protective League, an organization composed of "representative colored citizens of Saline county," met and adopted resolutions denouncing the school, labeling Alston a traitor to the race and unfit to lead and deeming him unworthy of confidence. The league also condemned the actions of the attorney.

Throughout the summer of 1902, the board met several times at different locations and out of town to determine the fate of the school. The board decided to relocate the school. Cairo and Metropolis were sites under consideration. The case against the man charged with leading the riots was thrown out on technicalities, despite the violence and property destruction. The college was forced to close, and almost all Black residents left the city. One newspaper reported that Deacon Wade and Isham Ray were the last Blacks to leave town.

In August 1902, the board voted to relocate the school to Metropolis and reopen there. In January 1903, the board adopted resolutions thanking the governor, president, the AME church and individuals for their actions. Some newspapers reprinted the correspondence from the governor to the school and to the sheriff.

J.D. Alston relocated his family to Metropolis, but the school did not reopen. In June 1912, Alston delivered the commencement address at Frederick Douglass School in Marion, Illinois. He died in 1920, and his death certificate lists his occupation as printer. The site of the Eldorado Normal and Industrial Institute was demolished in 1994 due to termite infestation.

INGRAM HILL

A meeting was held on October 25, 1862, in Harrisburg to discuss bringing in contraband Negroes as laborers and domestics. A motion was adopted to remove them from Saline County.

Whereas the constitution of Illinois prohibits negroes and mulattoes on granting to and settling within, the State, and Whereas numerous hordes of contrabands have been sent within the limits of the State, which we regard as an infringement upon State rights, and whereas a number of said contrabands have been recently brought within the limits of Saline County, contrary to the wishes of a large majority of the citizens…Resolved. That we the citizens of Saline County, in mass assembled, respectfully ask that said contrabands be sent or taken without the limits of the county forthwith. Resolved that if any other person has in contemplation to bring more of said contrabands into the county, in the name of the constitution and humanity to desist the thought at once.

Ingram Hill was the Black settlement in Harrisburg. In 1873, the Harrisburg AME circuit comprised Redwood, Galatia and Williamstown. In 1878, the AME conference appointed Geo. H. Haithman to the Harrisburg circuit. The Pleasant Baptist Church began in Thomas Clark's home in 1875. Reverend Richard Price is credited as organizing the church in 1880. Reverend Driver dedicated the church when it occupied the building at South Main and Church Streets, the former home of the First Baptist Church, sometime between 1884 and 1896. Will Graves pastored the church around 1921, when it moved to North Main and Elm.

Image of Lewis Sanitorium Harrisburg, Saline County. *Private collection of Jeanne Mays.*

Reunion for Harrisburg School class of 1922, May 19, 1986, Saline County. *Front, from left to right*: Archie Stewart and Harvey Lee Fields. *Back, from left to right*: Augustus Pringle, Charles Patton, Ralph Towles and Nathaniel Stone. *Private collection of Gladys Burnett.*

Historical markers at 407 and 517 East Walnut Street mark the home of James Henry Lewis and the Lewis Sanitorium, which he built in 1927. Dr. Lewis was a graduate of Meharry Medical School (class of 1922). He married nurse Ruby Lanton in 1933. The couple treated patients in the community, and the hospital operated until the 1960s. Dr. Ross is mentioned as a colored physician who practiced in Harrisburg in the 1930s, and he likely worked with the Lewis family.

Archie Stewart is an alumnus of Lincoln School in Harrisburg. He is pictured in the accompanying photo alongside his classmates in the class of 1922. The photo was taken on May 19, 1986, at a class reunion event. Photographed are Archie Stewart, Harvey Lee Fields, Augustus Pringle, Charles Patton, Ralph Towles and Nathaniel Stone. Oscar Easton was one of M.D. and Sarah Easton's children. Oscar lived in Harrisburg with his wife, Carrie. M.D. was married to Hazel Phillips at the time Oscar died at age forty-two on October 14, 1937. Oscar Easton is one of many Black residents buried in Sunset Hill Cemetery in Harrisburg.

LAKEVIEW

The Lakeview settlement formed sometime after the War of 1812. Early references called it the Pond Settlement or Cypress Pond, because of its location. The Mt. Zion Baptist Church was formed in 1869. On July 24, 1886, land was deeded to Thomas Allen, Josiah Taborn and Joseph Cole, trustees of the Mt. Zion Baptist Church, probably for a new building. The building closed in May 2000, and the last pastor to hold services there was Ownly Williams. Lakeview Cemetery remains active, with more than 163 surnames and approximately 50 newborns and stillborns buried there. Of those buried there, the oldest was born in 1798 and the youngest in 2000. Black veterans of the Civil War, the Spanish-American War, World War I, World War II, the Korean War and the Vietnam War are interred there.

Other churches that were part of the Lakeview settlement include the Lakeview Church of God on East Washington and Baber Chapel AME.

Right: Lakeview community sign in Carrier Mills, Saline County.

Below: Lakeview Cemetery and Church, Carrier Mills, Saline County.

Lakeview Church Bell, Saline County.

Lakeview Cemetery, Saline County.

Death certificate for Elvira Allen, burial at Lakeview Cemetery, Saline County.

Baber Chapel started in the home of Irvin (also spelled Ervin) Allen on his farm. Allen was born in North Carolina and lived with his siblings in Locust Grove before settling in Lakeview. The church closed in 2013, but the Allen descendants continued the custom of observing Decoration Day both in Lakeview and Locust Grove.

Dunbar School was established in a log building that burned in 1896. The school was rebuilt in 1900 and named Lakeview. In 1908, it was located at East Harrison and Allen Streets. William Archie Jones became the principal in 1924. The school burned again in 1930 and was rebuilt. Beatrice Anderson and John L. Taborn were among those who taught at

This is the remaining foundation of former Lakeview School, Saline County.

the school. Lakeview consolidated with Carrier Mills School in the 1956–57 school year. The school building is no longer standing. Only the foundation remains and is visible from the road.

Guardians of the Lakeview Legacy

Jewell Russell Cofield (1937–2018) and Nona Taborn are two daughters of Lakeview who are considered guardians of its legacy. Cofield was a local legend, having been the first to author a book documenting the Black settlement of Lakeview. *Memories of Lakeview* was the inspiration for many. The book inspired generations to trace their family history and their links to this historical site. Lakeview was home to many families with the surnames Allen, Cole, Taborn and others. In an interview for the Reclaiming the African American Heritage of Southern Illinois Project (RAAHSI), Cofield, at age ninety-nine, discussed her life growing up in Lakeview.

"My grandmother lived next door to us. We played Hide and Seek. We went swimming and fishing." She spoke of her favorite teachers,

The guardians of Lakeview Legacy: Nona Taborn (*left*) and Jewell Russell Cofield, in Saline County. *Private collection of Nona Taborn.*

John L. Taborn and Nancy Lanton. She said the school was integrated in the early years. "I don't think Black children and the white children knew the difference. They were mulattoes." She said her parents, Arnett Russell and Violet Dabbs Russell, were strict Baptists. "We went to Sunday School every Sunday." Her father, born in Princeton, Indiana, worked for the coal mines and as a carpenter. When an injury prevented him from working in the trades, he raised rabbits and chickens and sold them. "We lived off the land," Cofield said. Though she did not recall personally meeting Sarah Breedlove (Madam C.J. Walker), three generations of Jewell Cofield's family—her mother, herself and her daughter Lois—attended beauty school. She and her mother attended Walker's beauty school; her daughter attended Poro, the beauty school of Annie (Turnbo) Malone, who was born in Metropolis.

Nona Taborn is the author of the *Lakeview Keepsake Book*. The book builds on the foundation documented earlier by Cofield and highlights the achievements of many Lakeview descendants. The daughter of Freda Marietta Portee and Hayward Jones, Taborn also grew up with her grandparents as her neighbors.

Taborn recalled: "Some of my favorite pastimes and enjoyment were just riding in the backseat of my father's car while he shot rabbits and squirrels to bring home for my mother to cook. Picking blackberries, mulberries, plums, persimmons, apples, peaches, and all kind of goodies, grew in abundance, free for the picking." She was first inspired to write in high school and recalls being encouraged by her English literature teacher. She graduated from the Southeastern Illinois School of Nursing. After beginning her career in nursing, she married Rickey Taborn in 1974, and they had three children. After her family grew to four grandchildren and two great-grandchildren, she returned to give birth to the dream that became the *Lakeview Keepsake Book 2016–2017*. "I have lived in Carrier Mills for most of my life and feel that the decision to raise my family in the small town that I was raised in was a good decision. This is my happy place."

SOUTH AMERICA

South America was home to South America Missionary Baptist Church, which served as the school and cemetery. The following is an excerpt from a poster from November 23, 1850, advertising for the capture and return of a runaway.

$150 REWARD! RAN AWAY from the subscriber a negro man named Patrick. He left on the 21 of July last, a dark copper color and will weigh a hundred eighty or one hundred ninety pounds, about thirty-four or thirty-five years old, five feet and seven inches tall, round shoulders and heavy made. He has a few marks on his right side near the shoulder, caused by a whip from patrols. He has a down look when spoken to, a high forehead and a small bald place on his head, very polite, he is extremely fond of liquor and can read print a little, make coarse shoes and can cooper very well, a good basket maker and can bottom chairs very well. Also, a handy fellow with tools about a farm. He was raised in Bedford County, Tennessee…and was sold to me in February last. He and his wife. He has very short hair and close to his head and had on heavy whiskers when he left home.…When last heard he was in the state of Illinois, Saline County inquiring for a free negro by the name of Jackson. He was in four miles of Jackson's. The settlement is called South America in consequence of the free Negroes in it.

16

UNION COUNTY

The first evidence of Blacks in Union County was a court case brought by "Milly, a black woman." In 1818 and 1820, there were people recorded having enslaved persons or servants in their household, but there were no free persons of color in either record. In 1818, Blacks accounted for 39 of a total county population of 2,485. In 1820, they were 22 of 2,384. Though the accounts vary, the number of Blacks as a percentage in the county never reached 1 percent, whether enslaved person, servant or free person. Union County maintained a Negro registry and taxed one dollar for every Negro brought into the county.

An enslaved man named George was purchased in Jefferson County, Arkansas, in August 1836 and brought to Union County and hired out. George filed his freedom suit in September 1838 and gained his freedom on December 2, 1839. Though slavery was said to have ended in the county in 1845, in 1853, a law was enacted preventing Blacks from coming into Illinois and staying more than ten days. The law was not repealed until 1865. In 1863, many people were arrested and charged for bringing Blacks into Union County.

The families credited as settlers in Union County are the Allen, Bass, Brown and Ivey families. "The only regular Negro settlement in the county is in this precinct. Arthur Allen, a wandering son of 'Africa's golden strand,' was among the early settlers here. He has gathered around him a number of his people, thus forming quite a colony of the 'bone of contention' between the North and the South."

Arthur and Patience (Hawley) Allen and Joseph and Elizabeth Ivy arrived in 1828. The following year, Beverly and Adaline (Abernathy) Brown settled. By 1835, there were forty-seven Blacks in the county. Arthur and Patience are recorded on the census at age fifty-five with their children. When Arthur Allen's estate was probated, there were provisions for his children's education, which suggests the existence of a subscription school for Blacks in the settlement. One source places the "Allen settlement "on the eastern side of the county, northeast of Mt. Pleasant.

Thomas and Elizabeth Bass and their children came to Illinois before 1850. Thomas Bass, a Black physician, is named and shown as living in Union County on the tax list in 1854, the state census in 1855 and the federal census. On the 1870 and 1880 censuses, he is recorded living in Cobden. In March 1857, Dr. Bass was arrested and charged with the rape of a white woman. The charges were dropped. He was released, and the case was never tried. Members of the Bass family also lived in Jackson and Williamson Counties.

Joseph Ivy was living in Franklin County in 1818. By 1820, he was the head of household in Franklin County. He moved his family to Union County, because he was paid to build a bridge, which he finished in December 1834. In November 1837, he sold his farm and left Union County. The Ivy settlement came to an end after two of its residents were indicted for a plan to murder a nearby "racist politician." The charges were dropped, but Ivy (Ivey) and his friends had moved on by the 1840 Census. The 1850 Census records the following last names: Allen, Algers, Bass and Bateman. The oldest resident was Thomas Bass, sixty-eight; the youngest were two one-year-olds, Jane Allen and an unnamed female Bass child.

The Black settlements were located in Cobden (South Pass) and Makanda (North Pass). The Cobden settlement was known as South Pass, where the South Pass / Cobden Cemetery was located. In most cases, the school and church were simply referred to in the way the August 17, 1872 *Jonesboro Gazette* reported: "The colored citizens of Cobden intend on holding a barbecue at that place for the benefit of the colored church." In 1875, a schoolhouse was built in the Black settlement of South Pass.

Beverly Brown married Hannah Parham. They settled in Union County in 1829 with their four children: Addison (twenty-eight), Minerva (twenty-six), Robert (twenty-four) and Louisa (twenty-one). Beverly died on April 1, 1839. Addison died on April 17, 1849. Robert died on July 31, 1858.

There are a few documented cases of Blacks being baptized or admitted into white churches, but the majority are believed to have established their own church. According to the history of Rockhill Baptist Church, it was first formed in Makanda about 1871 in the Black settlement called Toppington (Topping Town). The church was founded by members of the Bass, Denton (or Benton) and Matthews families. Pastors Benton and Orr were the organizers. A short time later, Rockhill Church "moved" to Carbondale (Jackson County). Though the church no longer exists, there is a Toppington/Walker Cemetery in Union County.

A review of a sample of death certificates shows a high number of Blacks buried at the Anna Insane Hospital Cemetery. The January 6, 1912 edition of a local newspaper reported a man's recent commitment to the Anna Hospital for the insane. "This is the sixth person to be adjudged insane within the last month, and the second out of six to lose his reason over religion."

Anna Jonesboro expelled Blacks through mob violence in 1863 and 1909. "In 1863 a mob of 25 men led by an Anna doctor forced 40 black residents out of town." The 1863 incident involved Black Civil War veterans who were brought to town from Cairo to work on a farm. Local citizens objected to their use as a cheaper labor alternative and forced their return.

17

WHITE COUNTY

The first land patents in White County were not issued until 1815, but Black people were likely already there. The 1818 census records the following free persons of color: Milly Bonny, Henry Brawdy, Joshua Davis, Jesse Day, Samuel Day, Frederick Hammons, Drury Harrison, Levi Morgan, Catherine Rawlings and William Roace. By 1840, the number of Black heads of households had declined. Only Robert Baker, David Brumit, Drew Harris and Hester McCoy were listed.

According to the 1850 Census, the oldest living Black in the county was William Anderson, seventy, a mulatto born in Pennsylvania. The youngest was three-month-old Alexander Buckner. The surnames on this census are Anderson, Baker, Beacher, Bozeman, Buckner, Burress, Cherry, Chism, Ford, Freeman, Green, Grunter, Hammons, Hardin, Harris, King, Lorgenfree, Madison, Orenton, Parker, Smith, Stoggins and Wilson.

The Black settlements were located in Carmi and Grayville. Maple Ridge and Sand Hill (Saw Hill) were the cemeteries. One historian, in *History of White County*, reports the formation of an AME church in 1868 under the administration of Reverend George Benson, with W.B. Hammonds as pastor and Henry Williams as class leader. A new building was erected in 1881 at a cost of $600. Reverend Eli Lane organized another Methodist church in 1878. Frank Hinton was the pastor and Henry Sherman the class leader.

The *History of White County* also states: "Free Will Baptist Church was organized several years ago [before 1881] by Reverend Abraham Rice who died in March 1881. Ministers Bryant Smith and Willim Driver pastored the church that was located North of Main Street on the bank of river in East Carmi. Church members were: John White, Joseph Abel, Simon Edwards, Madison Allen, Morgan Allen (clerk) and Mr. Barker (secretary).

"The frame schoolhouse for colored children was built in 1874 on lot 53, East Carmi, two squares north of Main and one square east of the river, at a cost of about $1,000."

The 1850 Census provides some insight into Black settlement in White County. O. Cherry, a twenty-one-year-old mulatto male from Illinois, resided in the home of a surveyor from Pennsylvania. Thomas Hardin, a thirty-two-year-old mulatto blacksmith, was head of household 37–37 with his wife, Menerva. Also in the household were William Hardin (three), Lucretia Hardin (two) and Henderon King (seventeen), from Georgia. Menerva was from Tennessee, and the other Hardin children were born in Illinois.

Harry Chism, a Black farmer from Tennessee, was a thirty-year-old head of household with a twenty-four-year-old female, Elizabeth, and a six-month-old named George. Elizabeth and George are listed as mulatto. Household number 454, with George and Nancy Hayas, is listed as a Black household. George and Nancy were listed as seventy and sixty-three, respectively. George is listed as a farmer from Maryland, and Nancy was from Virginia. Elizabeth Ford, fifty-two, was a rare Black female head of household. Born in Virginia, Ford lived alone.

Number 566 is the mulatto household of Beverly Hammons (twenty-five), a male born in Illinois. His occupation is listed as laborer. Also in the household were Fannie (twenty-three), born in Indiana, Eliza (four) and Theodore (one). Fielding Masion (twenty-eight) is a farmer from Tennessee. His household consisted of Nancy (twenty-five), from Virginia; Malissa (three), born in Indiana; and Articia (one), born in Illinois.

18

WILLIAMSON COUNTY

B lack settlement in Williamson County began in Franklin County, when enslaved Blacks arrived in Cave Township between 1804 and 1820. Land entries were first recorded in 1814. That year, one source says, "a man by the name of Elliott, partially colored was stabbed and killed." The year after Williamson County was formed, the 1840 Census lists Black households headed by John Ellis, Daniel Russell, Solomon Russell and Rhuben Scelton (Skelton). The total population of the county was 4,457, with 29 free Blacks.

Rachel Watson was kidnapped from her family's farm in Locust Grove. In 1844, the postmaster wrote a letter requesting assistance in locating her. In 1851, a man was indicted for kidnapping a colored child, Mathilda, near Carbondale. In 1857, Susan Whiteside was kidnapped near Marion.

The 1860 Census records Black residents with the following last names: Bryant, Ellis, Gray, Hardeson, Hardison, Harrison, Hopkins, Killian, Martin, Miller, Mitchell, Overton, Renfrow, Scott, Sides, Skelton, Stewart, Storey, Walden and Wiley. The oldest Black resident was eighty-four-year-old Milly Miller in the household of a "white" Miller family. She was born in Virginia about 1776. The youngest Black resident was four-month-old Marvine Wiley.

Shaffer Chapel AME Church, Dewmaine/Colp, Williamson County.

Black settlements in the county were located in Colp, Dewmaine, Marion, New Denison and Thompsonville. The Black settlements in Colp and Dewmaine formed around 1898, when Blacks were recruited to work in the nearby no. 9 mine. The derogatory term was "Negro nine." Colp Cemetery, Shaffer Chapel AME Church and Mt. Olive Missionary Baptist Church were institutions in the settlement.

DEWMAINE

Dewmaine was one of a few Black settlements to have its own physician. Andrew Welton Springs was recruited to the area in 1908 by Reverend C.C. Phillips of the local Baptist church. Dr. Springs, an Eagle Scout, launched the first Black Boy Scouts troop. Birdie McLain, also a physician, was his wife. Birdie Springs was Native American, but sources conflict on the tribe, either Cherokee or Comanche.

Dr. Springs later went on to work for the coal mine and developed a respirator called the pulmotor. He used it to save lives when the mine exploded in 1914. He treated Blacks and whites in the community, and he was often mentioned in local papers and are collected in the book *Events in Egypt*.

Dr. Springs, colored physician at Dewmaine, had been summoned the day of the drowning. Finding the boy had not been recovered, he jerked off his clothing and plunged into the river. When he brought him to the banks, Dr. Springs applied his pulmotor in vain effort to bring back his life. 11 Aug 1917.

Dr. AW Springs of Dewmaine, reports there are four other cases (Pelegra) in the county, including one colored one.

Dr. McLain Springs of Dewmaine has a beautiful beaded hunting bag which is an heirloom in family. Dr. AW Springs exhibited this beautiful piece of beadwork in Marion on Tuesday and stated that it had been owned in his wife's family for many years and that none of the present generation knew its age. Dr. McLain Springs is a member of the Comanche tribe of Indians. Dr. Springs has written to the US Department of the Interior to see if he cannot arrange for a representative of the Comanche tribe to come to this county to take part in the exercises at the schools on Labor Day. This has been set by the Illinois Legislature for Friday September 24 and exercises will be held at the schools in recognition of the day.

A published announcement of Dr. Springs's political candidacy in 1918 enumerated his many accomplishments. It appears in *Events in Egypt*.

The announcement has been made of Dr. AW Springs of Dewmaine, a candidate for the Republican nomination for member of the Illinois Legislature for the 50th senatorial district. The following regarding his is from the book Who's Who of the Colored. *Andrew Welton Springs, physician and surgeon, was born at Charlotte, NC November 22, 1869, son of Thomas & Mary Ann Springs. He was educated in the public schools of Durham S.C. and was given a B.S. degree at Fisk University at Nashville, TN. In 1901, also given a M.D. Degree at National Medical University of Chicago in 1906, and is a graduate of Illinois Mine Rescue and First Aid Commission station Benton, Illinois. Studied helmet work and given certificate by the American Mine Safe Association of Pittsburg, PA in 1914. Married Birdie E. McLain M.D.….Three children, Pearl E. Deceased, Fannie and AW Jr. Began practicing in Chicago in 1907; physician and surgeon to Madison Coal Corporation of Dewmaine since 1912; physician in charge of the corporation hospital, medical lecturer…first physician, white or colored to pass examination as prescribed by Illinois Mine Rescue Commission, director Dewmaine public schools, served as sergeant and member hospital corps to Illinois National Guard. 1906–1908, is a Republican, Episcopalian, fellow American Medical Society member, William County Medical Society member, member committee on first and American Mine Safety Association. Mason, member Odd Fellows, Knights of Pythias, American Red Cross, First Aid Division.*

The street where he lived, Washington Street, was renamed A.W. Springs Drive on May 15, 1976, in honor of his contributions to the community.

The Dewmaine and Colp settlements are also known for the accomplishments of many of its residents. Jimmy Springs, son of A.W. and Birdie Springs, was a member of the singing group The Red Caps. The group signed a studio contract in 1956. Just as his father did not live to see Jimmy's rise to fame, Jimmy died in 1987 in Philadelphia before the group was inducted into the Vocal Group Hall of Fame in 2007.

Arvelle Riggins was born in Colp in 1900. Riggins played in the famous Negro Leagues for the Detroit Stars, among other teams. James L. Kirby

Dr. A.W. Springs, circa 1915. Williamson County. *Private collection of Duane Perkins.*

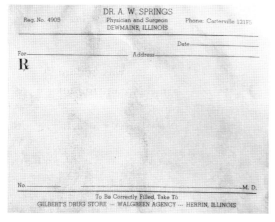

Left: Dr. A.W. Springs's prescription pad. Williamson County. *Private collection of Duane Perkins.*

Right: Memorial for miners lost in mine explosion, Williamson County.

Death certificate for John William Allen, signed by A.W. Springs. Williamson County.

and Archibald Mosley were among the first Blacks to train in North Carolina and serve during World War II as Montford Point Marines. After military service, Reverend Mosley pastored Shaffer Chapel Church. He also served as teacher and principal at Attucks Grade School. William Dewayne Perkins is the elder of the settlement and maintains an archive of the settlement's history and works to ensure its preservation.

While many greats were born in Colp and Dewmaine, the settlements also experienced their share of violence. On June 30, 1889, the owner of the mine brought a contingent of Negro miners and their families from Pana to work his mine during the third strike at the mine. The

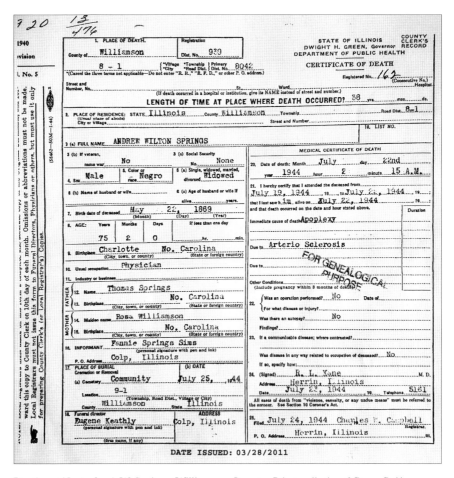

Death certificate for A.W. Springs. Williamson County. *Private collection of Duane Perkins*.

train carrying the miners and their families was attacked at Lauder (now Cambria). One Black woman was killed, and twenty people were wounded. In 1899, white miners drove Black strikebreakers out of Carterville.

Junior Hatchett's and Cowboy Town were local hangouts. They were open only on weekends, and there was a separate place for teenagers. Local gatherings received more than their share of negative press. The following was collected in *Events in Egypt*:

> *Mrs. Anna Hamilton shot Walter Powell, a gambler, at No. 9 north of Dewmaine. The trouble was over the ownership of a suitcase. Both*

Top, left: Colp, No. 9 Dewmaine, Williamson County. Hometown Heroes Riggins and Springs.

Top, right: William Duane Perkins, 2022. Colp/Dewmaine, Williamson County.

Bottom: Colp Memorial Plaza honoring local veterans. Williamson County.

Example of a poster recruiting Blacks to work in mines. *Private collection of Duane Perkins.*

are Negroes as white in color as most white persons. He is thought to be mortally wounded and she is in jail. Thursday 6 Jun 1912.

James Garrett, colored constable at Dewmaine, was shot to death there Thursday. He went down under the fire of Will Lee, colored, who for years it is said, has threatened to "get Jim Garrett," and who but recently returned to the county with an avowed intention of carrying out his threat. Lee made his escape. Hardly had the echoes of the shooting died away, when an Italian…opened fire, said to have been wholly unwarranted, upon a passing a negro, Bud Bridges, known as Buster Bridges. He was instantly

Death certificate for Walter Harrison, burial at Dewmaine Cemetery, Williamson County.

killed. On Thursday, Garrett had brought four alleged bootleggers to the county jail....Returning to Dewmaine, he was told Will Lee and Frank Clarica alias Clarence Clair, two drunken negroes, were on the warpath. He deputized two or three Negroes, one of them John Dudley, and went after them. During the shooting, Clarica was wounded and it is believed he cannot live. Garrett is said to have slain eight men in his life, all of them Negroes. He was never punished, but was tired once here and acquitted (a lengthy account) 11 Sep 1914.

Mrs. Eliza Cook 67 year old colored woman, died Tuesday at the county farm. She has no relatives except her husband whose whereabouts are unknown. Burial was Wednesday. 8 Aug 1917

MARION

Marion's Black settlement was Freeman Spur. In 1857, a "Negro girl living near Marion was kidnapped and people rallied and brought her back." Blacks lived in a section that was later called the Gent Addition. The cemetery was Rose Hill, and the church was Bethel AME.

The Bethel AME sixteenth anniversary booklet tells the history of the church, located at 308 South Monroe. It was organized in November 1887. Reverend Stokes was the full-time pastor. Charter members were Anna Mathews, Sabra Gray, Sara Gray, Reverend Thomas King, Ellis Waddles, Joe Allen, Mr. and Mrs. Ogletree and Mr. and Mrs. Bird. The prior building was on East Main and North Madison Streets. Construction on the lot on East Main began in 1900. The Monroe Street building was erected in 1903 under the leadership of Reverend Alex Chavis. H.R. Hackley pastored from 1915 to 1918.

The Ockletree members of Bethel AME Church likely included Henry Ockletree, whose crime and punishment was publicized in the local paper. He probably was not alive when the following was printed, as recorded in *Churches of Williamson County*:

Thirty-five years ago, the Egyptian Press said, "Upon a close calculation it is said the case of Henry Ockletree, colored, now confirmed in the county jail for sixty days, will have cost the county over $125 by the expiration of his punishment. He was convicted of stealing two hogs valued at $14. Of course, there is at present no remedy for such an enormous expense to punish petit larceny, but it does seem that a more effectual penalty with less expense attached could be devised by our law makers." 13 Jun 1912

The church was also the original site of the school. During his tenure, Reverend Douglass served both as minister of the church and teacher at the school. Miners built their own store that later became a black school, it was named Douglas honoring both the current pastor and the historical abolitionist. The orator for the 1912 commencement was J.D. Alston,

Scale and deli slicer belonging to Milton Allen from his store in Marion on Copeland Street. *Private collection of Garry Allen.*

who was known for his efforts launching the Eldorado Normal and Industrial Institute, which closed due to racial violence. Mrs. Joe Jackson, nineteen, wife of the Goodhall Hotel porter, died Monday of tuberculosis. Funeral services will be held at the ME church, Colored, by Reverend Fred Douglas, with burial in Rose Hill. 19 Dec 1912

Freeman Spur was no different from the other settlements in that it saw racial violence. The Herrin Massacre was a labor dispute with racial undertones. When the miners decided to strike, the owner brought in fifty strikebreakers and their families. A Black woman died and many were wounded when the protestors shot up the train car that was bringing them to town. As recorded in the book *Herrin* by Scott Doddy: "A man born in White County, wrote to a publication, the Monitor, saying that he got a job teaching at colored school near Marion said he 'has had many attacks from enemies swearing that no man shall live in this neighborhood and teach Negroes…some said he would not live to get a month taught,' and he feels his life is in danger."

ELLISVILLE

Gravestone of Missouri (Scott) Ellis, New Denison / Ellis settlement, Williamson County.

The references to a Black settlement in Creal Springs likely concerns the Ellis settlement, as it was established before New Denison was incorporated. Some publications called it Seaburg (1879). It has also been referred to as Locust Grove in sources stating that the Methodist church located in Creal Springs was moved. New Denison was named after a physician who owned land but never lived there. The cemetery is often referred to as the Ellis Cemetery or Ellis and Toney (Tony) Cemetery, after the people who are buried there. In addition to Ellis and Toney, the names Lucas, Johnson, Sneed and Harris appear on the tombstones. Many of their deaths were reported in local papers and are collected in *Events in Egypt*.

> *Robert Johnson, colored, is on trial for the murder of "grasshopper" Sneed. He shot Sneed on Election Day and Sneed died from the effects of his wound. Johnson was one of the few Democratic Negroes in Southern Illinois. Sneed was in an auto with a party of other colored people, when he hopped from the car running toward Johnson, being given a beating because of his standing up for Dunne. Tuesday 27 Mar 1917*

> *About 11 o'clock Thursday evening unknown parties planted a bomb at the northeast corner of the bath house in the Ozark Park in Creal Springs. The entire east side of the city felt the jar of the explosion, but other than scattering some dirt and blackening the weather boarding near where it exploded no damage was done. The explosive was made by wrapping rope around a sack of powder. The bath house contains the sleeping quarters of the colored help at the hotel and the action is supposed to be the outcome of bitter feelings against the Negroes here. 9 Jun 1913.*

John Ellis was a Revolutionary War veteran whose gravestone served as a memorial in the cemetery. A historical marker along the road indicates

1. PLACE OF DEATH	STATE OF ILLINOIS	COUNTY CLERK'S RECORD

County Williamson — State Board of Health - - Bureau of Vital Statistics

Registration Dist. No. 3738 — STANDARD

Township or Road Dist. — Primary Dist. No. — **CERTIFICATE OF DEATH**

Incorp. Town or Village or City Marion — No. 1009 South Madison St.; Ward — Registered No. 16

[If death occurred in a hospital or institution, give its NAME instead of street and number.]

2. FULL NAME Missouri Ellis

PERSONAL AND STATISTICAL PARTICULARS

3. SEX F

4. COLOR OR RACE Black

5. SINGLE, MARRIED, WIDOWED, OR DIVORCED (Write the word) Married

6. DATE OF BIRTH June-22, 1858 (Month) (Day) (Year)

7. AGE 58 yrs. 7 mos. 25 ds. If LESS than 1 day, ... hrs. OR .... min.?

8. OCCUPATION (a) Trade, profession, or particular kind of work Housewife (b) General nature of industry, business, or establishment in which employed (or employer)

9. BIRTHPLACE (State or country) Ill.

10. NAME OF FATHER Robert Hundley

11. BIRTHPLACE OF FATHER (State or country) Ill.

12. MAIDEN NAME OF MOTHER Scott

13. BIRTHPLACE OF MOTHER (State or country) Ill.

14. THE ABOVE IS TRUE TO THE BEST OF MY KNOWLEDGE

(Informant) Claude Ellis

(Address) Marion

15. Filed Feb-18, 1917 Bert Scobey, Dep. Registrar

MEDICAL CERTIFICATE OF DEATH

16. DATE OF DEATH Feby-17, 1917 (Month) (Day) (Year)

17. I HEREBY CERTIFY, That I attended deceased from Jan-27, 1917 to Feb-16, 1917, that I last saw her alive on Feb-27, 1917, and that death occurred, on the date stated above, at 5 P.m.

The CAUSE OF DEATH* was as follows: I believe it was Cardiac Dropsy.

FOR GENEALOGICAL PURPOSE

(Duration) yrs. mos. ds.

Contributory (Secondary)

(Duration) yrs. mos. ds.

(Signed) G? J. Parmley, M. D.

(Address) Marion

Date Feb-19, 1917 Telephone 279

18. LENGTH OF RESIDENCE (For Hospitals, Institutions, Transients, or Recent Residents): At place of death yrs. mos. ds. In the State yrs. mos. ds. Where was disease contracted, if not at place of death? Former or usual residence

19. PLACE OF BURIAL OR REMOVAL New Dennison

DATE OF BURIAL Feb-19, 1917

20. UNDERTAKER Cash and Scobey

ADDRESS Marion

*State the DISEASE CAUSING DEATH, or, in deaths from VIOLENT CAUSES, state (1) MEANS OF INJURY; and (2) whether ACCIDENTAL, SUICIDAL, or HOMICIDAL.

Above: Death certificate for Missouri (Scott) Ellis, burial at Ellis Cemetery, New Denison, Williamson County.

Opposite, top: Death certificate for Reverend William Douglas Harris, burial at Ellis Cemetery, New Denison, Williamson County. Harris was likely the pastor of the church in the settlement.

Opposite, bottom: Historical marker, Ellis Cemetery, New Denison, Williamson County.

the site of the cemetery, which lies between two homes on private property. Rocha (Allen) Harris married W.D. Harris, and both are buried in Ellis Cemetery. Mr. Harris was a minister and likely pastored the church in the settlement, whose name is unknown.

Locust Grove

The Locust Grove settlement in Thompsonville began before the county was formed, in the Cave Township of Franklin County. A brochure touting its attractions stated, "There are no colored or foreign people in Thompsonville and no saloons or 'bootleggers.'" The accuracy of that statement is doubtful, since the presence of Blacks from the earliest times of Franklin County is well documented. More famously known as Africa or Fancy Farm, the settlement was renamed Locust Grove when the post office was moved to Williamson County.

Many individuals have been credited as settlers of Locust Grove. Among these are Priscilla (Silla) McCreery and her husband, Richmond (Richard) Inge (also spelled Eng, Enge and Ing). The two are recorded in census records in Franklin County, and this would seem to support the claim that McCreery and Inge were early settlers if not the founders of the Black settlement.

Another assertion is that the "negro family Stewarts (from Kentucky) were freed by their master and given forty acres of land for each family. They took their former owner's name." This claim is doubtful, because the "Black" Stewarts of this settlement were born in Tennessee. In 1850, they were in the census in Missouri as the only free Black family in the county. Their arrival in Southern Illinois likely occurred between 1851 and 1860, long after the area was established. Timothy Stewart, the patriarch of the Stewart family, served in the Civil War and is buried in Locust Grove Cemetery with a family headstone with his first wife, Aby Rebecca Harrison, and a military headstone.

The Harrison family, though not credited as one of the settlement's founding families, maintained a large presence there. The Harrisons did come from Kentucky, where some of them had been enslaved.

Locust Grove has also been referred to as Skeltontown, probably because of an elder resident, Reuben Skelton. In the 1860 Census, the seventy-five-year-old is a resident of Williamson County. Also called Negrotown, at its height, Locust Grove was home to a church, a school and two cemeteries. The Old Locust Grove Cemetery was the first of the institutions to fall into disrepair. The only documented people interred in this cemetery are Ephrain/Ephraim and Winey/Winney Jones. The couple married in Gallatin County in 1837. Ephraim died in 1866 at age fifty. Winey died in 1851 at thirty-seven.

Locust Grove Cemetery is an active cemetery where most of the settlement's residents and descendants are interred. Other names that refer

					Illinois Federal Census Report									

Secretary of State and State Archivist
1850 – 1860 – 1870 – 1880
Director of Archives

County Williamson   Township 8 South Range 4 East Post Office Fitts Hill

Date July 5, 1860   Page 1007   Line 26-40

Dwelling Number	Family Number	NAME (all mulattos)	Age	Sex	MONTH BORN (70, 80 only)	Relation to family head (80 only)	OCCUPATION	PROPERTY Real (50, 60, 70 only)	Personal (60, 70 only)	Md. within yr.	Parents of Foreign Birth (70 only) Fa. Mo.	BIRTHPLACE	FATHER'S BIRTHPLACE (80 only)	MOTHER'S BIRTHPLACE (80 only)
1604	1436	Skelton, Rubin	75				Farmer	1400	180			N. Carolina		
		Skelton, Martha	60									Virginia		
		Gray, Leonard	14									Illinois		
1606	1438	Hopkins, (sh?dy)	65	M			Farmer	150				Virginia		
		Hopkins, Jane	47									Kentucky		
1606	1438	Stewart, Joel	54?									Tennessee		
		Stewart, Aggy	30									Illinois		
		Stewart, Joel	7									Illinois		
		Stewart, Margaret	5									Illinois		
		Stewart, George	2									Illinois		
1608	1437	Martin, Presley	26				Farmer	1600	550			Virginia		
		Martin, Susannah	58									Virginia		

AR 0-11.1   Jefferson

This 1860 Census shows listing of "Mulattoes" in Locust Grove, Williamson County.

to the same cemetery are Allen Cemetery and Parke Chapel. Sherwood Thomas Williams, who died on October 8, 1878, of cholera, is listed as buried in the "African Church."

Richmond Inge is recorded receiving eighty acres in 1872. He later gave land to the AME church. On April 20, 1880, Richmond conveyed an acre of land to the trustees of Allen Chapel: Sufeo Long, Morris Stewart, Elbert Harrison, Lewis Harris and Henry William.

AME conference proceedings of 1873 mention home missions of Allen Chapel, suggesting the church formation was prior to the widely published 1890 date. The church in the settlement was Allen Chapel AME, but it is unclear whether it was named for the Allen residents who made their home there or for Bishop Richard Allen, the founder of the AME church denomination. Those who served as pastors of the church over the years included Howard Harrison, Henry Williams, George Long, Burl Hammon, Benjamin Moss and Reverend Haithmon. Beatrice Corley became pastor in 1943, and the church was rebuilt in 1944. When it could no longer stand due to vandalism, the church was demolished in the 1980s.

VETERAN OF CIVIL WAR DIED SUNDAY

Timothy Stewart, New Dennison Colored Soldier, to Be Buried Wednesday.

Timothy Stewart, colored veteran of Union army service in the Civil War, died at his home at New Dennison, at 2:30 a. m. Sunday.

Deceased was born in Tennessee, and was 86 years, three months and seven days of age.

He served in Company E, 29th Regiment, U. S. Colored Infantry in civil war.

He was married Oct. 3, 1872, to Abbie Harrison. Eight children born to that union survive. They are Mrs. Let Story, Aaron Stewart, and William Stewart of Marion, Mrs. Tilda Allen., Thompsonville, Charles of Youngstown, Ohio, Mrs. Rose Shackley, Indiana, and Mrs. Sarah Adams, Oakland, California.

The first Mrs. Stewart died 30 years ago. Mr. Stewart was married a second time seven years ago to Alice Jones who survives his death.

During his active life, Mr. Stewart followed the occupation of farming. He was a member of the A. M. E. church here.

Mr. Stewart came to Illinois 70 years ago and had lived in Williamson county for the last sixty years. Hew as a member of the I. O. O. F. and G. A. R. of Carmi.

Funeral services Wednesday at 2 p. m. at Park Chapel in Locust by Rev. Leander Miller of 's Mill.

Above: Newspaper obituary for Timothy Stewart, a Civil War veteran. Williamson County.

Opposite: Land grant to Richmond Inge, Locust Grove, Williamson County.

When Jesse Gray's wife, Jane, died in 1892, many residents of the settlement were named in a foreclosure suit attempting to evict them from the land. Years before, Jane Gray, who was the widow of Shandy Hopkins, married Jesse Gray, when they were both fifty-nine. The plaintiff's lawsuit proved unsuccessful, and Jesse was able to remain on the land with his wife's family, due to evidence and testimony provided by Jane's grandson Charles Shelby. This outcome is perhaps the motive behind Jesse Gray's death the following year. The published report stated his cause of death, at the age of seventy-eight on May 14, 1893, as "thrown from a cart in a runaway, caused concussion & compression."

Though the first Blacks to settle are unclear, among them were the children of Susannah Martin. She was emancipated in Virginia and recorded as free with her children, Catharine, Permelia, Presley, America, Melinda and Obedience. Permelia and Catharine would marry on the same day in 1844 and settle with their respective husbands. The other siblings settled in Locust Grove.

The Martins are ancestors of the Bean and Craig families. Ary Dimple Bean is an alumnus of the Southern Illinois Normal University (now SIU), class of 1924. She married Roy Craig and raised her family in Harrisburg. Ary wrote of Locust Grove.

The chief occupation was farming. Tobacco and castor beans were the chief crops. They were marketed at Marion, Galatin, and Carbondale. Castor beans brought $1.50 a bushel, and tobacco sold for $3 and $5 per hundred and top quality brought $6. They always took a white man with them to market, because the buyers would not give a Negro a fair price. My

280

The United States of America,

To all to whom these Presents shall come, Greeting:

Whereas, In pursuance of the Act of Congress, approved September 28th, 1850, entitled "An Act granting Bounty Land to certain Officers and Soldiers who have been engaged in the Military Service of the United States," Warrant No. *6235* for *80~* acres, issued in favor of *George Lawson, Private in Captain Sangsters Company Virginia Militia War of 1812*

has been returned to the GENERAL LAND OFFICE, with evidence that the same has been duly located upon the *North half of the North West quarter of Section Thirtyfive, in Township Seven South, of Range Four East, in the District of Lands Subject to Sale at Shawneetown Illinois, containing Eighty acres*

according to the Official Plat of the Survey of the said Lands returned to the *GENERAL LAND OFFICE* by the SURVEYOR GENERAL: *Which has been Assigned to Richmond Inge*

Now Know Ye, That there is therefore granted by the UNITED STATES unto the said *Richmond Inge*

the tract of Land above described: TO HAVE AND TO HOLD the said tract of Land, with the appurtenances thereof, unto the said *Richmond Inge and to his*

heirs and assigns forever.

In Testimony Whereof, I, *Franklin Pierce*

PRESIDENT OF THE UNITED STATES OF AMERICA, have caused these Letters to be made Patent, and the SEAL OF THE GENERAL LAND OFFICE to be hereunto affixed.

GIVEN under my hand, at the CITY OF WASHINGTON, the *Second* day *of January* in the year of our Lord one thousand eight hundred and *fiftyfour* and of the INDEPENDENCE OF THE UNITED STATES the seventy-*eighth*

BY THE PRESIDENT: *Franklin Pierce*

By *Jno. Ho. Wheeler Asst* Sec'y.

[SEAL]

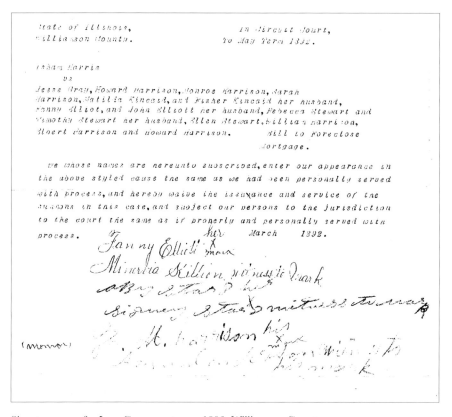

Signature page for Jesse Gray court case, 1892. Williamson County.

grandmother was widowed and had a family of 10 to raise. She raised sheep and had a loom, and taught the daughters to card and spin and weave. Each family raised his cotton and carded it for the quilts. They raised their own food, and canned and stored it for winter, and took their corn to the mill to be ground for feed and meal. In time they built two churches and a Negro school was started, taught by Negro teachers. When no Negro teachers were available, it was taught by white teachers. Sometimes there were as many as 40 Negro children enrolled, and sometimes a few white children who lived near came to it. This was very unusual for white children to attend a Negro school, and especially one taught by a Negro teacher. For recreation, church festivals were held, usually every 2 weeks on a Saturday night. The women baked pies and cakes, fried chicken, and made ice cream, and sold candy and chewing gum. These were attended by almost everyone in the community, who was not too sick to come, or too old to walk so far. The

Tax receipt for Presly Martin, tax year 1880. Williamson County. *Private collection of Toni Craig Garrison.*

church held quite a prominent place in the community, and anyone who failed to come or to send his children to Sunday school was looked down upon or considered "different" from the other folk. Play parties, as they were called, were quite popular. At these parties, the Virginia and other folk dances were "played." They were played to the accompaniment of singing, hand clapping, and stomping. Sometimes, rarely a fiddle was used. Dancing was taboo, as the old folks were very strict moralists. Having attended many of these myself, I know these people were only dancing to singing. But I have never yet talked to one who would admit that they were dancing. Some of the songs used were, "Old Billy Logan," "Shortening Bread," "So Mr. Brown," "Ain't Goin' to Rain No Mo," and many other folk songs. At these parties almost every food imaginable that was grown on the place was served and sometimes each family would bring a contribution. Songs were sung, and all kinds of games were played, like "Spin the Plate, Post Office, and Rail Road Car" were played. Not only the young participated, but the old as well. I have seen my father, in his sixties, stomp and sing through the Virginia reel many times, and my mother will play it yet as quickly as I will, and she has almost reached her three score and ten. In 1937, there remained only seven families living in this community. I was born and raised here, and both my parents live here now. There still remains one church which has only nine members, and there has been no Negro school for more than 40 years. The children attend the white district school.

BIBLIOGRAPHY

"Ad Colors History of South America. Saline County, Illinois." *SAGA* 32, no. 4: 21.

Aiken, H.M. *Franklin County History*. Centennial Edition. Prepared for the Franklin County Centennial Committee, 1918.

Alexander County, Illinois. 1850 Census. Transcribed by Maxine E. Wormer. Thomson, IL: Heritage House, 1973.

Alexander County Profiles: A Compilation of Essays on Alexander County History. Cairo High School Students, Woman's Club and Library Association of Cairo, Illinois, 1968.

Allen, John W. *It Happened in Southern Illinois*. Carbondale: Southern Illinois University Press, 1968.

———. *Legends & Lore of Southern Illinois*. Carbondale: Southern Illinois University Area Services Division, 1963.

Annotated 1860 Census, Massac County, Illinois. Transcribed by Pauline Artman, David Artman and Colleen Norman. Evansville, IN: Evansville Bindery, 1992.

Benton III Commercial Club. *The Prospects of Franklin County, Illinois, 1912*. Benton, IL: Hammond Press, 1912.

"Bethel AME Carbondale 1864–2014." 150th Anniversary Booklet. Carbondale, Illinois, 2014.

Bethel AME Church, Carbondale, Illinois.

The Biographical Review of Johnson, Massac, Pope & Hardin Counties Illinois, Containing Biographical Sketches of Prominent and Representative Citizens. Chicago: Biographical Publishing Company, 1893.

Blackman, W.S. *The Boy of Battle Ford and the Man*. Carbondale: Southern Illinois University Press, 2012, 19, 28, 71.

Bonifield, Elaine. *Alexander County Cemeteries. Alexander County, Illinois*. Cairo, IL: Cairo-Egyptian Adult Center, 1976.

Brief History of Rock Hill. 150th anniversary publication. N.p.: 2021.

Carlson, Shirley J. "Black Migration to Pulaski County, Illinois 1860–1900." *Illinois Historical Journal* 80, no. 1 (Spring 1987): 37–46.

Centralia (IL) Sentinel. "House at Tamaroa Holds Secrets of Fleeing Slaves." May 3, 1966.

Collard, Ami. "Randolph County Servitude & Emancipation Records 1809–1863." *Illinois State Genealogical Society Quarterly* 29, no. 1: 9–28.

———. "Randolph County Servitude & Emancipation Records 1809–1863." *Illinois State Genealogical Society Quarterly* 28, no. 4: 236–44.

Commercial Press (Cairo, IL). "Alexander County Profiles." No date.

Cox, Anna-Lisa. *The Bone and Sinew of the Land: America's Forgotten Black Pioneers and the Struggle for Equality.* New York: Public Affairs, 2018.

———. *A Stronger Kinship: One Town's Extraordinary Story of Hope and Faith.* Lincoln: University of Nebraska Press, 2006.

Crowder, Lola Frazer. 1850 Census of Randolph County, Illinois. N.p.: 1998.

Davis, James E. *Frontier Illinois.* Bloomington: Indiana University Press, 1998.

Dexter, Darrel. "Birth Records 1882–1899, Pulaski County, Illinois." *SAGA* 31, no. 1: 36.

———. *Bondage in Egypt: Slavery in Southern Illinois.* Cape Girardeau, MO: Center for Regional History, Southeast Missouri State University, 2011.

———. "Estray Book 1835–1839, Union County, Illinois." *SAGA* 39, no. 1: 8–9.

———. *A House Divided Union County, Illinois 1818–1865.*

———. "Records of African Americans and American Indians Alexander County." *SAGA* 27, no. 1: 45–52.

———. "Runaway Slave Records: Cairo Newspaper Accounts Alexander County, Illinois." *SAGA* 28, no. 4: 51–56.

———. "Runaway Slave Records Cairo Newspaper Accounts Alexander County, Illinois Part 2." *SAGA* 29, no. 1: 3–7.

———. "Slave Records and Freedom Papers Courthouse Documents 1809–1863, Randolph County, Illinois." *SAGA* 29, no. 2: 3–25.

———. "Slave Records in Alexander County." *SAGA* 18, no. 2: 35–38.

———. The Slave Register. Gallatin County, Illinois.

———. "Ullin Cemetery, 1856–2001, Pulaski County, Illinois." *SAGA* 28, no. 2: 3–19.

———. "Union County Estray's Book O." *SAGA* 18, no. 2: 39.

———. *Union County, Illinois Cemeteries.* Carterville, IL: Genealogy Society of Southern Illinois, 2003.

———. Union Grove Cemetery Pulaski County, Illinois: 56–63.

Douglas, Mary Nelle. Hardin County, Illinois, 1840–1850 U.S. Census.

———. Hardin County, Illinois, 1860 U.S. Census.

Eifschneider, Mary. "Kimzey House near Tamaroa Historic Home Hid Slaves." *Southern Illinoisan* (Carbondale, IL), January 16, 1966.

1830–1840 Federal Census of White County, Illinois. Copied and indexed by Shirley J. Hannaford. Carmi, IL: White County Historical Society.

1840 Federal Census of Williamson County, Illinois. Transcribed and indexed by Helen Sutt Lind. Marion, IL: Williamson County Historical Society.

The 1850 Federal Census of Johnson County, Illinois. Transcribed and indexed by the Tri-City Genealogical Society. Richland, WA: Locust Grove Press, 1973.

The 1850 Federal Census of Saline County, Illinois. Transcribed and indexed by The Tri-City Genealogical Society. Richland, WA: Locust Grove Press, 1973.

1850 Federal Census of Union County, Illinois. Copied and indexed by Bernice C. Richard. Chicago: self-published, 1976.

1850 United States Census of Franklin County, Illinois, with Annotations. Transcribed by Frank and Carol Rademacher. Mt. Prospect, IL: Frank Rademacher, 1977.

1860 Federal Census & Mortality Schedule of Pope County, Illinois. Transcribed and indexed by Ricky T. Allen. Decatur, IL: Bowers Press, 1983.

1860 United States Census of Hamilton County, Illinois. Copied by Frank and Carol Rademacher. Mt. Prospect, IL. Printed by Frank Rademacher, 1977.

Ekberg, Carl J. *French Roots in the Illinois County. The Mississippi Frontier in Colonial Times.* Champaign: University of Illinois Press, 1998.

Ford, Thomas. *A History of Illinois: From Its Commencement as a State in 1818 to 1847.* Urbana and Chicago: University of Illinois Press, 1995.

Franklin County History. Reprinted from Aikin, *Franklin County History.*

Franklin County Illinois and Its Development.

Frost, Vickie. *Murphysboro Illinois 150 Years: A Pictorial History, 1843–1993.* Murphysboro, IL: Jackson County Historical Society, 1994, 44, 70, 74, 77, 134.

Gallatin County, Illinois, 1860 8th United States Census. Transcribed by John V. Murphy and Mrs. Mary Afton Anderson. Carrier Mills, IL: John V. Murphy.

Gallatin County, Illinois, Federal Census of 1830. Published by the Saline County Genealogical Society with permission from Judy Winget. Mulkeytown, IL. Originally copied by Mrs. Mary Afton Anderson, 1976.

Goodwin, Ruby Berkley. *It's Good to Be Black.* Carbondale: Southern Illinois University Press, 1953.

Grisham, Violet Lee Carter. *Williamson County Churches.* Vol. 1. Marion, IL: Williamson County Historical Society, 2019, 2, 5, 6.

Griswold, John. *Herrin: A Brief History of an Infamous American City.* Charleston, SC: The History Press, 2009.

Hardesty, Richard. "Descendants of Jesse Hardesty, Early Pioneer. Hamilton County, Illinois." *SAGA* 32, no. 4: 23.

Heerman, M. Scott. *The Alchemy of Slavery: Human Bondage and Emancipation in the Illinois Country, 1730–1865.* Philadelphia: University of Pennsylvania Press, 2018.

Historical Tour of Northeast Carbondale. September 23, 2002. Carbondale Planning Services Division.

History of Jackson County, Illinois: With Illustrations, Descriptive of its Scenery, and Biographical Sketches of Some of Its Prominent Men and Pioneers. Philadelphia: Brink, McDonough & Co., 1878. Duplicated by East Bay Blue Print & Supply Company. Oakland, California, 1973 and 1983.

"History of Shawneetown. The Oldest Living City in the State of Illinois." Annual celebration, July 1–4, 1961.

History of West Frankfort, Illinois. West Frankfort, IL: Frankfort Area Historical Society, 1978.

History of White County Illinois. Chicago: Inter-State Publishing Company, 1883.

Husband, Will W. *Old Brownsville Days: An Historical Sketch of Early Times in Jackson County, Illinois*. Reprinted 1973 by John W.D. Wright. Murphysboro, IL: Jackson County Historical Society, 1935.

Jackson County Album: A Photo Album of the Communities of Jackson County, Illinois. Murphysboro, IL: Jackson County Historical Society, 2006, 104.

Jefferies, Richard W. *The Archaeology of Carrier Mills: 10,000 Years in the Saline Valley of Illinois*. Carbondale: Southern Illinois University Press, 1987.

Jones, P.M., and Vickie Frost. *Forgotten Soldiers: Murphysboro's African-American Civil War Veterans*. Murphysboro, IL: Class Publications Committee; Papyrus Consultants, 1994.

Journal of the Illinois State Historical Society 27, no. 1 (1934).

Lansden, John M. *A History of the City of Cairo, Illinois*. Carbondale: Southern Illinois University Press, 2009.

Lantz, Herman R. *A Community in Search of Itself: A Case History of Cairo, Illinois*. Carbondale: Southern Illinois University Press, 1972.

Lawler, Lucille. *Amazing Shawneetown: A Tale of Two Cities*. Evansville, IN: Evansville Press, n.d.

———. *Gallatin County. Gateway to Illinois*. East St. Louis, IL: Saunders Printing Service, 1968.

———. *One Room Schools in Gallatin County, Illinois*. Evansville, IN, Evansville Bindery Inc., 1995.

Lind, Helen Sutt, comp. *Events in Egypt*. Vol. 1, *1856–1878*. Newspaper extracts, Williamson County. Johnson City, IL: self-published, 1994.

———. *Events in Egypt*. Vol. 2, *1879–1881*. Newspaper extracts, Williamson County. Johnson City, IL: self-published, 1994.

———. *Events in Egypt*. Vol. 3, *1882–1887*. Newspaper extracts, Williamson County. Johnson City, IL: self-published, 1994.

———. *Events in Egypt*. Vol. 4, *1888–1891*. Newspaper extracts, Williamson County. Johnson City, IL: self-published, 1994.

———. *Events in Egypt*. Vol. 5, *1894–1895*. Newspaper extracts, Williamson County. Johnson City, IL: self-published, 1994.

———. *Events in Egypt*. Vol. 7, *1899–1900*. Newspaper extracts, Williamson County. Johnson City, IL: self-published, 1994.

———. *Events in Egypt*. Vol. 8, *1901–1904*. Newspaper extracts, Williamson County. Johnson City, IL: self-published, 1994.

———. *Events in Egypt*. Vol. 10, *1910–1912*. Newspaper extracts, Williamson County. Johnson City, IL: self-published, 1994.

———. *Events in Egypt*. Vol. 11, *1913*. Newspaper extracts, Williamson County. Johnson City, IL: self-published, 1994.

———. *Events in Egypt*. Vol. 12, *1914*. Newspaper extracts, Williamson County. Johnson City, IL: self-published, 1994.

———. *Events in Egypt*. Vol. 13, *1915*. Newspaper extracts, Williamson County. Johnson City, IL: self-published, 1994.

———. *Events in Egypt*. Vol. 14, *1916*. Newspaper extracts, Williamson County. Johnson City, IL: self-published, 1994.

———. *Events in Egypt*. Vol. 15, *1917*. Newspaper extracts, Williamson County. Johnson City, IL: self-published, 1994.

———. *Events in Egypt*. Vol. 16, *1918*. Newspaper extracts, Williamson County. Johnson City, IL: self-published, 1994.

———. *Events in Egypt*. Vol. 17, *1919*. Newspaper extracts, Williamson County. Johnson City, IL: self-published, 1994.

———. *Events in Egypt*. Vol. 18, *1920*. Newspaper extracts, Williamson County. Johnson City, IL: self-published, 1994.

———. *Footprints in Williamson County, Illinois* 9, no. 2 (Summer 2006). Williamson County Historical Society.

Loewen, James W. *Sundown Towns: A Hidden Dimension of American Racism*. New York: New Press, 2005.

Lude, Max H. *The Historic Shawnee Trails: "Franklin County" Shawneetown to Kaskaskia & St. Louis Trails*. 2nd edition. Franklin County, IL: Franklin Area Genealogical Society, 2009.

"Massac County Genealogical Society. Records of Free and Freed African Americans." *SAGA* 27, no. 2: 24–29.

Massac County Illinois 1843–1987. Paducah, KY: Turner Publishing. 1987.

May, George W. *History of Massac County Illinois*. Galesburg, IL: Wagoner Printing Company, 1955.

———. *History Papers on Massac County*. Galesburg, IL: Wagoner Printing Company, 1955.

McLean, John. *One Hundred Years in Illinois, 1818–1918: An Account of the Development of Illinois in the First Century of Her Statehood*. Chicago: Peterson Linotyping Company, 1919.

Mitchell-Carnegie Public Library. *A History of Saline County and a Brief History of Harrisburg Illinois, 1853–1933*. Harrisburg, IL, n.d.

Montague, E.J. *A Directory, Business Mirror of Historical Sketches of Randolph County*. Alton, IL: Courier Steam Book and Job Printing House, 1859.

Moyer, W.N. *Moyers' Brief History of Pulaski County 1843–1943*. Mound City, IL: The Pulaski Enterprise, 1990.

Norton, Margaret Cross. Illinois Census Returns, 1810, 1818. Collections of the Illinois State Historical Library. Vol. 24. Springfield: Illinois State Historical Library, 1935.

———. Illinois Census Returns, 1820. Theodore Calvin Pease, Collections of the Illinois State Historical Library. Vol. 26. Springfield: Illinois State Historical Library.

Ogg, Louise P., and Monica L. Smith. *Alexander County Illinois*. Vol. 1, *1989*. Paducah, KY: Turner Publishing, 1989.

"Old Rose Hill Cemetery, Johnson County, Illinois." *SAGA* 26, no. 2: 17.

"One-Room Schools & More." Randolph County Genealogical Society, Randolph County Illinois. No date.

Page, O.J. *History of Massac County, Illinois*. Metropolis, IL: Massac County Genealogical Society, 1995.

Parks, George. *History of Union County with Some Genealogical Notes*, 1984.

Perry County Illinois. Vol. 1. *History of Perry County, Illinois 1827–1988*. Paducah, KY: Turner Publishing Co., 1988.

Perry County, Illinois 1860 U.S. Census. Transcribed by Lee Schick and Naomi Schick. Hood River, Oregon.

Pirtle, Carol. *Escape Betwixt Two Sons: A True Tale of the Underground Railroad in Illinois*. Carbondale: Southern Illinois University Press, 2000.

Pope County, Illinois 1986: History and Families, 1816–1986. Pope County Historical Society. Paducah, KY: Turner Publishing, 1986.

Pope County, Illinois. Vol. 2, *History and Families, 1816–1989*. Pope County Historical Society. Paducah, KY: Turner Publishing, 1989.

Proceedings of the Twelfth Session of the Illinois Conference of the African Methodist Episcopal Church held at Springfield, Illinois. Bloomington, IL: Mattoon Commercial Print, 1883.

Puckett, Martin, and Delores Puckett. *Census of White County, Illinois*. Decatur, IL: Decatur Genealogical Society, 1972.

Pulaski County Illinois 1860 Federal Census. Transcribed and published by Brenda Weatherington Jenkins. 2nd ed. Grand Chain, IL, 1994.

Ramsey, Susie M., and Flossie P. Miller. *The Heritage of Franklin County Illinois*. Benton, IL: Benton Evening News, 1964.

Randolph County Illinois Commemorative Edition 1795–1995. Paducah, KY: Turner Publishing Company, 1995.

Rose, James M., and Alice Eichholz. *Black Genesis: A Resource Book for African-American Genealogy*. 2nd ed. Baltimore, MD: Genealogical Publishing Inc., 2003.

Rush, Linda. "Darrel Dexter Illuminates Cairo's Past." *Southern Illinoisan* (Carbondale, IL), January 23, 2011.

Russell, Herbert K. *A Southern Illinois Album: Farm Security Administration Photographs 1936–1943*. Carbondale: Southern Illinois University Press, 1990.

———. *The State of Southern Illinois: An Illustrated History*. Carbondale: Southern Illinois University Press, 2012.

Saline County, a Century of History Illustrated. Presented by the Saline County Historical Society as the Centennial book 1847–1947. Harrisburg, IL: Saline County Historical Society, 1947.

Seventh Session of the Illinois Annual Conference of the African M.E. Church Held at Alton, Illinois. Chicago: Birney Hand & Co, Printers, 1878.

Shaffer Chapel AME, Colp, Illinois.

Shaw, Louis. *History of Carrier Mills*. Vol. 2. Carrier Mills, IL: Carrier Mills-Stonefort Public Library District, 2022.

Spirit of Attucks Burnett Devers Breakfast Program, July 2, 2016. Carbondale, Illinois.

United States Census 1850, White County, Illinois. Copied by Martin Puckett and Dolores Puckett. Decatur, IL: Decatur Genealogical Society, 1986.

Waterloo (IL) Republican, June 22, 1899. (Pinckneyville teacher salaries.)

Wilcox, J.F. *Historical Souvenir of Williamson County Illinois*. Effingham, IL: LeCrone Press, 1905.

Williamson County Illinois Death Records. Vol. 1, 1877–1886. Transcribed by Charla Schroeder Murphy and Helen Sutt Lind. Marion, IL: Williamson County Historical Society, no date.

Williamson County Illinois Death Records. Vol. 2, 1885–1903. Transcribed by Charla Schroeder Murphy and Helen Sutt Lind. Marion, IL: Williamson County Historical Society, no date.

Williamson County Illinois Sesquicentennial History. Compiled by Stan J. Hale. Carterville, IL: Turner Publishing Company, 1993.

Wright, John W.D. *A History of Early Carbondale, Illinois: 1852–1905*. Carbondale: Southern Illinois University Press for Jackson County Historical Society, 1977.

———. *Jackson County, Illinois Residents in 1850*. Carbondale, IL: Jackson County Historical Society, 1972.

ABOUT THE AUTHOR

Courtesy Jesse Torre Photography.

The author was inspired to write about her ancestors' Black settlements, and through research she discovered much more. This book only scratches the surface of the rich history of Black settlements in Southern Illinois. Kimberly France is a graduate of Howard University in the District of Columbia and of Southern Illinois University in her native Carbondale.